Power-Glide Children's German

Parent's Guide

by

Robert W. Blair

with

Dell Blair

This product would not have been possible without the assistance of many people. The help of those mentioned below was invaluable.

Editorial, Design and Production Staff

Instructional Design: Robert Blair, Ph.D., Dell Blair

Project Coordinator: James Blair

Development Manager: Erik D. Holley

Story Writer: Aaron Eastley

Cover Design: Guy Francis

Contributing Editors: Aaron Eastley, Erik D. Holley

Assistant Editors: Krista Halverson, Sean Healy, Ingrid Kellmer

Voices, Audio Cassettes: Jana Adams, Martha Beddoes, Richard DeLong, Björn Farmer, Antje Farmer, Amy LeFevre, Marcie McCarthy, Greg Peterson, Dathan Young

Illustrators: Krista Halverson, Apryl Robertson

Translators: Robert Blair, Dell Blair, Björn Farmer, Antje Farmer, Ingrid Kellmer

Music: SYNTH Sound Recording, Stock-Music.com

Audio Recording, Editing and Mixing: Geoff Groberg

© 1999 Power-Glide. All rights reserved.
Printed in the United States of America
ISBN 1-58204-036-2
PN 3221-01 (11/99)

No part of this publication may be reproduced, stored in a retrieval system, or transmitted, in any form or by any means, electronic, mechanical, recording, or otherwise without the prior written permission of Power-Glide.

Power-Glide Foreign Language Courses
1682 W 820 N, Provo, UT 84601

Contents

Introduction	P-v
Adventure: Visiting Cousin Max	P-1
Familiar Phrases	P-6
Adventure: Hike Down the Old Mill Stream	P-9
Match and Learn	P-13
A Girl and a Rat	P-17
Adventure: A Treasure Map	P-27
Lines and Figures	P-28
Adventure: Meeting Heidi at the Market	P-35
Colors at the Market	P-40
Adventure: Animals at the Zoo	P-49
A Boy and a Bear	P-52
Adventure: Making Gingerbread Men	P-61
Body Parts	P-63
Adventure: Harvesting Yams on a Farm	P-75
The Farmer and the Turnip	P-77
Adventure: Hungry Hunters Head Home	P-95
A Hungry Giant	P-96
Adventure: Visiting the Hermit of the Island	P-115
The Keys to the Gates of Rome	P-117
Adventure: Surprise Party	P-123
The Broken Window	P-125
Adventure: Flying Home	P-143
Dieter's Challenge	P-145
Adventure: Auf Wiedersehen!	P-159
Recipes	P-161

A Note to Parents

Basic Course Objectives

The major goal of this course is to get children excited about communicating in another language. The adventure story, the variety of activities, and the simplified teaching methods employed in the course are all designed to make learning interesting and fun.

This course is primarily for children Kindergarten through 4th grade. Course activities are designed specifically with these learners in mind and include matching games, story telling, speaking, drawing, creative thinking, acting, and guessing—all things which children do for fun!

Ultimately, children who complete the course can expect to understand an impressive amount of German, including several common German phrases, some complete German sentences, German numbers, colors, and body part words, and instructions for drawing and acting given in German. They will also be able to understand stories told all or mostly in German, to retell these stories using German themselves, and to make up stories of their own using words and sentence patterns they have learned.

Children who complete the course will be well prepared to continue learning at a more advanced level, and they will have the foundation that will make learning at that level just as fun and interesting, albeit more challenging than in this course.

Teaching Techniques

This course allows your children to learn by doing: to learn through enjoyable experiences. The idea is to put the experience first and the explanation after. This is important to note because it is directly opposite to how teaching—and especially foreign language teaching—is traditionally done. Typically foreign language teachers spend the majority of their time explaining complex grammar and syntax rules, and drilling students on vocabulary. In this traditional mode, rules and lists come first and experience comes last. Learning experientially, on the other hand, simulates the natural language acquisition process of children.

When children learn their native languages apparently effortlessly in early childhood, it is not through the study of grammar rules and vocabulary lists. Rather, they learn the words for things around them simply by listening to others, and they intuitively grasp an amazing amount of grammar and syntax in the same way. By using activities that simulate natural language acquisition, it is not only possible, but normal for children to learn a new language quickly and enjoy doing it!

Specifically, this course motivates your children to learn German by providing learning experiences in the form of matching games, story telling exercises, drawing exercises, singing and acting, and other fun activities aimed at developing functional language comprehension and speaking ability. These activities contrast markedly with the exercises in more traditional courses, which tend to focus exclusively on learning some vocabulary, or on understanding very simple German sentences, without extending learning to the point of actually understanding and speaking the language. Significantly as well, the language your children will acquire through this course will be more useful to them than language learned through traditional approaches, because knowledge gained in fun rather than stressful ways is much easier for children to retain and much more natural for them to use themselves.

Using the Course

This course is carefully designed so that it can be used either by children working primarily on their own or by parents and children working closely together. Complete instructions, simple enough to be easily followed by children, are included on the tapes. However, to get the most out of the course, parents should use the thorough written instructions provided in the *Parent's Guide*. The *Parent's Guide* page or pages for each exercise state exercise objectives, provide instructions for students and teaching tips for parents, and give a full audio transcript. Using these helps, parents or other adults can enhance the course significantly by acting as facilitators: reviewing instructions, encouraging creativity and course participation, providing frequent opportunities for children to display what they have learned, rewarding effort and accomplishment, and providing enthusiasm. Keep in mind that much of the real learning takes place as you interact with your children during and after the course learning experiences.

Using the resources provided in the course book and *Parent's Guide*, an adult learning facilitator does not need to know German or how to teach it in order to be a great learning partner. In fact, one of the most enjoyable and effective ways to learn is together, as a team.

Parents or other adults who know German can, of course, supplement the materials in this course very effectively. A proficient bilingual facilitator could, for example: (1) help children learn additional vocabulary by putting several objects on table and asking and answering questions about them, such as "What is this?" or "Where is the _____?", and so on; (2) create on-the-spot diglot-weave stories by reading illustrated children's books, putting key words (picturable nouns) into German, and asking questions about the story or its pictures partly or completely in German; (3) involve children in making and doing things (such as making a paper airplane or finding a hidden object) giving instructions all or partly in German.

Benefits of Second Language Acquisition

Learning a second language has many benefits. Besides the obvious value of being able to understand and communicate with others, research in the United States and Canada in the 1970s and '80s has shown that learning a second language gives children a distinct advantage in general school subject areas. Seeing linguistic and cultural contrasts as they acquire a second language, children gain insight not only into the new language and cultures, but into their own language and culture as well. Furthermore, a considerable amount of research has shown that learning a second language in childhood helps children learn to read and write their native language.

Our Goal

Our goal at Power-Glide is to change the way the U.S. studies language. We want to help people really understand and be able to use foreign languages, not just study them. This *Children's German Course* effectively launches children into understanding and being able to use German. We hope you and your children will find delight in the adventure of learning another language.

Visiting Cousin Max

This section contains an audio transcript of the adventure story your children will hear on the tape.

Instructions for This Page

Have your children listen carefully as the adventure story is read on the tape. Also, encourage your children to take an active part in listening to the adventure story. Ask them to respond to things they hear and have them say out loud words said by the characters on the tape.

Younger children might enjoy coloring the picture as the adventure story is read. Older children may want to follow along with the written audio transcript provided in this *Parent's Guide*.

Audio Transcript

 Narrator 2: The Adventure Begins: Visiting Cousin Max

Narrator: You and your sister Serena have been invited to visit your cousin Max and his family, who have recently moved to the main island of Papua New Guinea. On your first day there, Max takes you out in his yard to play with his big pet lizard. The lizard crawls around Max's shoulders and arms, and even up on his head.

Serena: Wow, Max, that's the biggest lizard I've ever seen, except in a zoo maybe. Watching it crawl around your shoulders is kind of creepy. Where did you get it?

Max: My dad brought it home for me last week. It's cool, huh?

Narrator: "Yeah," you say. "It's cool how its tail wraps around your neck, and how its tongue is always flicking in and out."

Serena: Yeah, and its scales are really bright green.

Narrator: "Can I hold him?" you ask.

Max: You bet, here you go.

Narrator: "Ouch!" you say. "His claws are really sharp! They're scratching my arms! Here, you take him, Serena."

Serena: Oh! It's like a cactus walking over your arm! You take him back, Max.

Narrator: But as Serena hands the big lizard back to Max, it gets frightened and jumps from her hands onto the ground and runs into the jungle.

Max: Hey, come back! Where you going?

Serena: It's running into the jungle! Hurry, or we'll never catch it!

Narrator: The three of you chase the lizard as it disappears into the jungle. As you run after the lizard, pushing past leaves and darting around tree trunks, you soon lose all sense of direction, and

Continued from Children's Activity Book, page 1

you're not sure how far you've run when Max finally says:

Max: Hey guys, I can hear the sound of a river up ahead! It must be the river my dad has told me about. He even has a raft down there somewhere that he's going to take me out in. Can you hear the river, you guys?

Serena: Yeah! It sounds like the water's moving really fast!

Narrator: "It is," you say. "I can see it now!"

Serena: I can see the river too. But Max, I haven't seen your lizard for a long time. Have you?

Max: No, but maybe if we get to the bank of the river we'll be able see them from there.

Serena: Good idea, Max. Come on, hurry you guys!

Narrator: The three of you continue running through the jungle, slipping on muddy ground as you get close to the river bank. As you approach the muddy, fast-moving river, you say, "All right, here we are. But where's your lizard, Max?"

Max: I don't know, I can't see him. Hey, wait! There he is! Down there on the other side of the river!

Serena: I see him! But how are we going to get to him since he's on the far bank? The water in this river is running really fast, and it looks really deep, too. I think if we try to wade across or swim, we'll get washed away!

Narrator: "Yeah, I think so too," you say. "But look you guys, there's something in the bushes down the bank by that big tree!"

Max: Yeah, it's kind of a steel gray color. Let's go see what it is.

Narrator: The three of you run down the river bank, trying to keep Max's lizard in sight, and trying not to slip on the mossy rocks that line the river bank. Serena gets to the thing first, and pulling back the branches from it, she says:

Serena: Look, you guys, it's a rubber raft!

Max: Wow, yeah. It must be my dad's raft! Look, there's just about enough room in it for the three of us! Using the raft, we could get across the river. I'm sure whoever owns it won't mind if we borrow it. We can bring it back when we are done.

Serena: OK. And since the water's running so fast, we could probably catch up with your lizard, too.

Narrator: "Do you think it's safe, though?" you say. "The water in the river's really muddy, and when our family has gone on river rafting trips dad has always told us that muddy water means dangerous water!"

Max: I don't know about you guys, but I'm going for it. I just got that lizard, and it's the coolest pet I've ever had. I'm not going to lose it now! So, are you guys coming or not?

Serena: I don't know, Max. It does look pretty fast. But we've gone river rafting lots of times, and we're good at it. I think we'll be all right.

Narrator: "I guess you're right, Serena," you say. "But let's be careful, and paddle to the nearest bank if we come to any rapids."

Max: That's a deal. Now, let's hurry or will never catch up to my lizard!

Narrator: The three of you pile into the raft and push off out into the main stream. Serena and Max each take a paddle, and soon you are rushing down the river and catching up to Max's lizard fast.

Max: Wow, this is great! At this rate, we'll catch him in no time!

Serena: Let's paddle over towards the other side, so when we get closer to your lizard we can get to the bank fast.

Max: All right, Serena, I'll paddle first to turn us that way, then you paddle to get us there.

Serena: Okay.

Narrator: "Hey, I see your lizard again, Max!" you shout over the rushing roar of the river. "But now it's on the bank we started from!"

Continued from Children's Activity Book, page 1

Serena: How did it get back over there?

Max: It must be able to jump from tree to tree across the river! Hurry, let's paddle back over to that side!

Serena: OK, I'll try, but the current in the middle of the river is really strong!

Narrator: As you try to paddle back toward the bank you started out from, your tiny raft is caught by the current and you are swept uncontrollably downstream.

Max: I can't steer anymore, you guys! The river is taking us down and we can't get out!

Serena: The current is just too strong!

Narrator: Powerless against the strong river current, you are swept downstream for what seems like hours. A few times as the river bends and curves you almost reach one of the banks, but at the last minute the current always sweeps you on, down stream. Just when you think you'll be carried along like this forever, Serena suddenly shouts:

Serena: Max! Do you hear that roaring sound up ahead? I think we're coming to some rapids!

Narrator: "Yeah!" you shout. "I think Serena's right!" Up ahead you now see the river dropping down into a deep canyon or gorge, with steep black cliff walls rising high on either side. "Paddle as hard you can, guys," you shout, "or we'll never make it!"

Max: All right, but now we're right out in the middle of the current! I don't think we can go to either bank before we get to the rapids! We're going to get pulled down through them! Hold on, you guys!

Narrator: Although Max and Serena paddle desperately to avoid it, the three of you get swept down the mainstream of the river into the middle of huge white rapids. You roll up over the top of towering waves, and down into deep boiling holes. Over and over again you are almost swamped. "This is crazy guys," you yell. "The waves are huge! These rapids must be class IV at least!"

Serena: Class V, I'd say!

Max: I don't care what class they are, I just want to get out of them! Hey, Serena, look out for that big rock! Paddle hard to the left!

Serena: I'm paddling, Max! But I think we're still going to hit it! Hold on tight, you guys!

Narrator: "Ow!" you scream as the raft hits the rock. "I can't hold on!"

Serena: Me neither!

Narrator: As your raft hits the rock, the three of you are thrown into the cold, muddy river. You come up gasping for breath and swimming hard to keep your heads above the water. With some effort you're able to get into slower water near the cliff walls at the sides of the canyon, but you're still being washed steadily downstream. A moment later the raft is washed free of the rock and is carried down the middle of the stream past you.

Max: <gasping and shouting> Hey, there goes the raft! Now what do we do?

Serena: <gasping> I don't think we have much choice! We're still being washed downstream.

Narrator: "I don't know about you guys," you say, gasping, "but I don't think I can swim like this for long. We have to find a way to get out of the river soon!"

Serena: Yeah, I'm already getting tired, too. But the cliffs here are way too steep to climb up or even to hold on to. We'll just have to keep swimming for a while!

Max: Uh-oh, you guys. I think we have a way bigger problem than that. Listen! Do you hear that roaring sound? I think we're coming to more rapids!

Narrator: "No!" you shout. "It isn't more rapids, it's a waterfall, just a little way up ahead! Look, the raft is getting swept over it right now!"

Serena: We're going to be swept over too! Oh, I hope it isn't a really long way down! Hold your breath, you guys!

Continued from Children's Activity Book, page 1

Narrator: The three of you, swimming desperately and at the last second each taking a big breath, are swept over the falls. You fall down, down, for what seems like forever. Then, with a SMACK, you hit the water below and plunge down, deep into the pool. The pressure in your ears is almost unbearable as you continue to sink deeper and deeper, the water from the falls pushing you farther and farther down. When the water finally stops pushing you down, you swim for the surface as hard as you can.

Just when you think you can't hold your breath any longer and your lungs are about to burst, you surge up out of the water and take a huge breath of air. The water is calm here, and you see Max and Serena already swimming toward the riverbank nearest you. Panting for breath, the three of you crawl up onto the bank, drenched from head to foot, but glad to be alive and out of the river at last. Gasping for breath, you say, "Wow, what a ride that was! I didn't think we'd ever make it through alive!"

Max: Me neither. Uh… I'm exhausted.

Serena: Me too…

Max: I wonder where we are now?

Narrator: "Yeah," you agree. "I think we must be miles and miles from your house, Max. We were swept down the river for a long time, and we were in the rapids for a long time too!"

Max: Yeah! Well, one thing is certain, we'll never get back home tonight. And even if we can find people near here to help us, they'll probably speak either Pidgin or German. Lots of people here in New Guinea speak Pidgin, and I remember dad saying that the river that runs near our house, goes through a big valley where everybody speaks German!

Narrator: "German?" you ask. "Why would they speak German here?"

Max: I don't know, but that's what he said. Maybe if we are in that big valley we can find someone who knows. If we can understand them!

Serena: But don't you know any German at all, Max? After all, you have been here for a few weeks. You must have picked up at least a little bit!

Max: Well, I have learned a few things, I guess. Some German is a lot like English even.

Narrator: "Really?" you say. "I don't think I know any German."

Max: I didn't think I knew any either, but then my mom told me some German words that we use in English too. For example, we call hotdogs Frankfurters sometimes, and when people sneeze we say Gesundheit, and those are both German words!

Serena: Huh! That's cool. Do you know how to say things like "Hello" and "Good morning" and "My name is" and stuff?

Max: Oh, sure, I can say those things. "Hello" is almost just like English. It's just *Hallo*.

Narrator: "*Hallo*," you say. "That is simple."

Max: Yeah, and "Good morning" is really easy to say too, it's just: *Guten Morgen*.

Serena: *Guten Morgen*. You're right, that is easy. What else do you know?

Max: Well, "Good day" and "Good night" are easy too. "Good day" in German is *Guten Tag*, and "Good night" is *Guten Nacht*.

Narrator: "So," you say, "when I meet someone here I can say *Guten Morgen* if it's morning, or *Guten Tag* in the middle of the day, or *Guten Nacht* at night!"

Max: Right on!

Narrator: "But then how would I introduce myself," you wonder out loud.

Max: To say "My name is" you just say: *Ich heiße* and then your name. So if I were introducing myself to someone I'd say, *Ich heiße Max*.

Narrator: "*Ich heiße Max*," you repeat.

Max: That's right, but put your own name in instead of mine.

Continued from Children's Activity Book, page 1

Serena: OK, I get it. So I would say, *Ich heiße Serena!*

Max: Right!

Serena: *Guten Nacht, Ich heiße Serena!*

Max: *Guten Nacht,* Serena. *Wie geht's Dir?*

Serena: "*Wie geht's Dir?*" What does that mean?

Max: It means, "How are you?"

Narrator: "How are you ... *Wie geht's Dir,* I can remember that," you say. "But what if after I introduce myself I want to ask the person I'm talking to what their name is? How do I ask that?"

Max: It's *Wie heißt Du?*

Narrator: "*Wie heißt Du?*" you repeat. "OK."

Serena: So, Max, *Wie heißt Du?*

Max: *Ich heiße Max.* And *Wie heißt Du?*

Serena: *Ich heiße Serena!* Thanks for teaching us those things, Max! I think you've learned a lot of German already!

Max: *Danke,* Serena.

Narrator: "*Danke.* Does that mean 'Thank you'?" you ask.

Max: Yeah! Good guess! And to say "goodbye" you say *Tschüß*.

Serena: *Tschüß! Danke,* Max! Well, what else do you know?

Max: That's about it so far. I can count to ten in German though. It's *eins, zwei, drei, vier, fünf, sechs, sieben, acht, neun, zehn!*

Narrator: "Say them again, Max," you say.

Max: OK. *Eins, zwei, drei, vier, fünf, sechs, sieben, acht, neun, zehn!*

Serena: I think I can remember those.

Max: Good. But now don't you guys think we'd better get going? If we don't find someone to help us soon, it will be dark, and we'll have to sleep out here in this forest!

Serena: You're right, Max. We'd better get going right away.

Narrator: "I think we should follow the river," you say. "Dad always taught us to do that if you're lost. There are always people living by rivers sooner or later."

Max: Sounds like a good idea to me!

Serena: Yeah, and we can review the German we've learned as we go along!

Familiar Phrases

This activity lets your children see how many of the German words and phrases from the adventure story they can remember. The narrator will read through the words and phrases twice, reading the German and then pausing for your children to say the English equivalent before giving the translation. Reading through twice will allow your children to review any words they don't remember during the first read through, and still be able to give the correct translation the second time.

Instructions for This Page

Have your children look at the German phrases in their activity books as they are read on the tape. During the pause after each German word or phrase is read, have your children say the English translation out loud.

If your children cannot remember some of the words, or give the wrong translation the first time through, simply let them listen to the correct answers given on the tape and try again during the second reading. If they still miss more than one or two on the second read through, let them rewind the tape and complete the entire activity again, with your help.

Audio Transcript

Narrator 2: Activity: Familiar Phrases.

Narrator: Let's review the new words and phrases Max taught you. As I say the words in German, try to say the right English words out loud. For example, if I were to say *Guten Tag*, you would say "Good day" out loud. OK? Let's try a few.

1. *Hallo.* Did you say, "Hello"? Good!

Corresponding Page from Children's Activity Book

Familiar Phrases

1. *Hallo.*	Hello.
2. *Guten Morgen.*	Good morning.
3. *Guten Tag.*	Good day.
4. *Guten Nacht.*	Good night.
5. *Ich heiße...*	My name is...
6. *Wie geht's Dir?*	How are you?
7. *Wie heißt Du?*	What's your name?
8. *Danke.*	Thank you.
9. *Tschüß.*	Goodbye.
10. *Eins, zwei, drei.*	One, two, three.

2

2. *Guten Morgen.* Did you say, "Good morning"? Very good.

3. *Guten Tag.* It's, "Good day", right?

4. *Guten Nacht.* You should have said, "Good night."

5. *Ich heiße.* Did you say, "My name is"? Good!

6. *Wie geht's Dir?* Did you say, "How are you?" Good.

7. *Wie heißt Du?* Did you say, "What's your name?" Good.

8. *Danke.* Did you say, "Thank you"? Good.

9. *Tschüß.* Did you say, "Goodbye"? Good.

10. *Eins, zwei, drei.* Did you say, "One, two, three"? Well done.

Were you able to say the correct English words? Good work! Let's go through the German words and phrases one more time. This time I'll just say the German words followed by the English words.

Continued from Children's Activity Book, page 2

1. *Hallo.* "Hello."
2. *Guten Morgen.* "Good morning."
3. *Guten Tag.* "Good day."
4. *Guten Nacht.* "Good night."
5. *Ich heiße.* "My name is."
6. *Wie geht's Dir?* "How are you?"
7. *Wie heißt Du?* "What's your name?"
8. *Danke.* "Thank you."
9. *Tschüß.* "Goodbye."
10. *Eins, zwei, drei.* "One, two, three."

How did you do that time? Better? Great! Now, let's go on with the adventure.

Hike Down the Old Mill Stream

This section contains an audio transcript of the adventure story your children will hear on the tape.

Instructions for This Page

Have your children listen carefully as the adventure story is read on the tape. Encourage your children to take an active part in listening to the adventure story. Ask them to respond to things they hear and have them say out loud words said by the characters on the tape.

 Younger children might enjoy coloring the picture as the adventure story is read. Older children may want to follow along with the written audio transcript provided in this *Parent's Guide*.

When your children get to the part of the adventure story where Nicole makes dumplings, stop the tape and turn to the Recipes section at the back of this *Parent's Guide* to find the recipe. Try making some!

Audio Transcript

 Narrator 2: The Adventure Continues: Hike Down the Old Mill Stream

Narrator: As dusk sets in, the seriousness of your situation does too, and the three of you start to really worry that you won't find anyone to help you. The thought of sleeping out in the forest at night, with all sorts of wild animals prowling about, is not good.

Serena: I hope we can find somebody to help us soon.

Narrator: "Me too," you agree, "I'm starting to feel really tired, and it's going to be dark soon." The three of you keep walking through the trees

Corresponding Page from Children's Activity Book

The Adventure Continues
Hike Down the Old Mill Stream

along the river. At last, just as it starts to get really dark, Max says:

Max: Hey look, you guys, there are lights up ahead. It looks like a house! And there's a big wheel thing in the river next to it!

Serena: Hey, yeah! It is light. The windows look really cheerful, glowing yellow in the dark. And I think I know why there's that big wheel thing in the river next to the house. It must be a mill house! That big wheel is a water wheel. The river makes it go around, and inside the house there's a big rock that grinds wheat and corn and stuff into flour. I saw a show on TV that showed how old fashioned mills work. It's really cool.

Max: That does sound cool. And maybe if the people here are nice, they will show us the millstone and let us sleep at their house tonight!

Narrator: The three of you knock on the door, and in a moment a friendly looking woman answers it.

Max: *Guten Nacht!*

Continued from Children's Activity Book, page 3

Nicole: *Guten Nacht. Kann ich euch helfen?*

Serena: What? I don't understand.

Nicole: Ah! *Sprecht ihr kein Deutsch?*

Max: No, we don't speak much German at all, yet. We speak English.

Narrator: "But we are learning German, though," you add.

Nicole: I see. Well, I speak some English myself, so let's talk in that for now. But what brings you here? Where did you come from and how did you get here? And why are your clothes damp? Have you been swimming in the river? Come in, please, and tell me what has happened to you.

Narrator: You all follow the woman into her home. She sits you down on chairs in her kitchen and you begin to tell her your story.

Serena: We came in a raft, down through the canyon! Our clothes are almost all dry again now, but after our raft swamped we did have to swim down the river for quite a while.

Nicole: Through the rapids and over the waterfall? I can hardly believe it! But here you are, so it must be true. Oh, my poor children, you must have been terrified! You're lucky to not be hurt.

Max: We know. It was really wild. But we made it, and now we don't even know where we are. Is this the valley where everybody speaks German?

Nicole: It is. I'm surprised you've heard of it. Not many people come here; our only regular contact with people from outside the valley is an airplane that flies in and out once each week.

Serena: Only once a week? You mean, we're trapped here until the plane comes?

Nicole: I'm afraid so. And it just came and left again yesterday, so it will be six days until it comes again.

Max: Six days! But my parents will be looking for us right away! They'll be really worried.

Nicole: Yes. Of course you're right. You'll have to go into the village first thing in the morning and contact your parents by radio. After that, though, I'm afraid you really are trapped here for a few days. You can, however, stay here with me and my husband Dieter until the plane comes again. I would love the company in the evenings, and you could explore our valley during the days! And now, we've got all this out of the way without introductions. I'm so sorry. My name is Nicole.

Narrator: "It's nice to meet you, Nicole," you say. Then you tell her your name, using some of the German Max taught you. Max and Serena introduce themselves too.

Max: *Ich heiße* Max.

Serena: And *Ich heiße* Serena.

Nicole: Wonderful! *Wunderbar!* You are learning German, I can see. I think you're doing very well.

Max: *Danke*, Nicole!

Nicole: You're welcome—*bitte*. Now let me see. The radio office is right in the middle of town, next to the market—*der Markt*. You can radio your parents and then stop in the market for lunch. That should be fun for you. In the market you'll meet people from all over our valley, and many from all around the world, even.

Narrator: "That sounds cool," you say. "But Nicole, why do all the people here speak German anyway?"

Nicole: It's quite simple, really. This valley was settled by German immigrants almost a century ago. There are still many people here who are descendents of those first settlers. And since then many other German speaking people have come here. The language you speak is always a great heritage to preserve. My own family came originally from Germany, and I still have relatives there.

Serena: Can you tell us about Germany, Nicole? I've never been there, and I'm not even sure what it's like!

Nicole: Certainly, Serena. I can tell you at least a bit about Germany, before Dieter gets home from work. Then when he arrives we can all have sup-

Continued from Children's Activity Book, page 3

per—if, that is, you all can help me make some dumplings for us to eat. Will you help me?

Max: You bet, Nicole. It sounds fun!

Narrator: Soon Nicole has all the ingredients out and you begin making dumplings as she tells you about Germany.

Nicole: Germany is a large country found right in the middle of Europe. There are three big rivers in Germany: the *Rhine*, the *Danube*, and the *Elbe*. Germans are famous for being hard workers, smart shoppers and smart people generally. They enjoy music, art, and philosophy, and they like to talk about those kinds of things. Soccer is Germany's most popular sport, and Germans like to hike and ride bikes and drive around to see things too. Germans like lots of different kinds of foods including potatoes, noodles, dumplings, vegetables, cakes, sausages, and chicken. These dumplings we're making right now are a German classic, in fact.

Serena: Wow, that's great, Nicole. Germany sounds like a neat place. If we can learn how to speak German, maybe we can visit there.

Nicole: It is indeed a fine place, and I'm sure you'd enjoy visiting. But Germany isn't the only place where people speak German, you know.

Max: What do you mean? Where else do they speak it?

Nicole: Well, there are, for example, many people who speak German in Switzerland, Austria, Luxembourg and Liechtenstein!

Narrator: "Wow," you say, "that's a lot of places. I never knew German was spoken outside of Germany either. That's cool."

Serena: Yeah. I hope we can learn a lot of German while we're here. After all, we'll be here for almost a week!

Nicole: If that is your desire, my friends, to explore this valley and learn some German, I think I have just the thing for you. Wait just one minute while I go and get it.

Narrator: Nicole leaves the room for a moment and comes back with an old piece of paper, yellow and cracking around the edges. Just as she reenters the room from one side, you hear someone open and close the front door to the house, and a man enters from the other direction. He stares at you, Max and Serena in surprise, and Nicole quickly explains.

Nicole: Ah, *Guten Nacht,* Dieter! My friends, meet my husband Dieter. Dieter, meet some friends who will be staying with us for a few days. They managed to make it through the rapids and safely over the waterfall, and now that they are here, they are planning to learn some German before they go home. I was just about to give them this.

Dieter: Ah, the map! *Sehr gute!* Well, my friends, it is a pleasure having you three in our home. I see that Nicole is already teaching you how to make dumplings!

Narrator: "Yeah, she is," you reply. "And she has been telling us about Germany! Is that where you're from too?"

Dieter: No, actually, I come originally from Switzerland, although in the part of Switzerland I'm from most people speak German. I can tell you a bit about Switzerland too, if you'd like.

Max: We sure would. It's cool to find out about far away places.

Dieter: Well, Switzerland is a beautiful country. In fact, many people consider it the most beautiful country in the world. In Switzerland there are many high mountains and lovely clear lakes. The country is sometimes called the "roof of Europe" because it is the home of a group of very tall mountains called the Alps. Most Swiss people work hard and they are almost always on time to things. Some of the best watches in the world are made in Switzerland. The Swiss people also like to play sports like soccer and to ride bicycles. They tend to be very active people and great lovers of nature.

Narrator: "Switzerland sounds really beautiful," you say. "Especially the Alps."

Adventure: Hike Down the Old Mill Stream — Hike Down the Old Mill Stream

Continued from Children's Activity Book, page 3

Dieter: The Alps are very majestic. And now, let's have supper. Also, I believe, Nicole has something else to give you.

Nicole: Indeed I do.

Narrator: The five of you sit around the kitchen table and enjoy a delicious supper. As you begin eating, Nicole takes out the old paper she had gone to get earlier.

Max: Hey, cool! It's a treasure map!

Nicole: Yes, Max, it is.

Serena: Yeah. But it's a strange one—look at all the Xs on it! Isn't there supposed to be just one X on a treasure map—the one that marks "the spot"?

Dieter: That's usually how it works, Serena, but this is a special map for finding a special treasure. At each spot marked on the map you'll find a part of the treasure you seek.

Narrator: "A part of the treasure," you say. "I don't get it."

Max: Me neither.

Nicole: I think you'll come to understand the treasure more and more as you go along, but for now, I'll give you the first clue or piece of the treasure, to get you started. It is: Build on what you already know.

Serena: Build on what you know? But what does that mean?

Dieter: Just what it says. If you're learning something new, like German, for instance, one of the best things to do right from the start is to build on what you know—to start by learning German words, for example, that are a lot like English words that you already know. Here, to explain it to you I'll teach you a couple of new words in German, and then I'll tell you a short story. How does that sound?

Max: Great!

Narrator: "Yeah," you say.

Match and Learn

This activity is visual, audio, and kinesthetic. It is designed to help your children learn by listening and pointing.

This first activity introduces the match and learn frames used frequently in this course.

Instructions for This Page

Have your children point to the picture as the tape directs.

 Younger children might enjoy coloring the pictures as the German words are said. Encourage your children to use these new words whenever possible. Make flashcards of the various pictures with the German words on the back and test your children regularly. Have your children create stories similar to the narrator's story at the end of the activity using these new vocabulary words.

Audio Transcript

Narrator 2: Activity: Match and Learn.

Narrator: Here are the things Nicole teaches you. First, as you already know, some German words sound a lot like English words. For example, the English word "ball" sounds a lot like the German word *Ball*. Listen again, you can hear how close they are: ball...*Ball*.

Another word that sounds almost the same in English and German is the word for soup. The German word for soup is *Suppe*. Just by knowing the English word soup, you could probably guess what the German word *Suppe* means.

One of the ways you can show that you understand words is by pointing to pictures when you hear words. Let's try it. Look at the picture boxes in your activity book and point to what you hear.

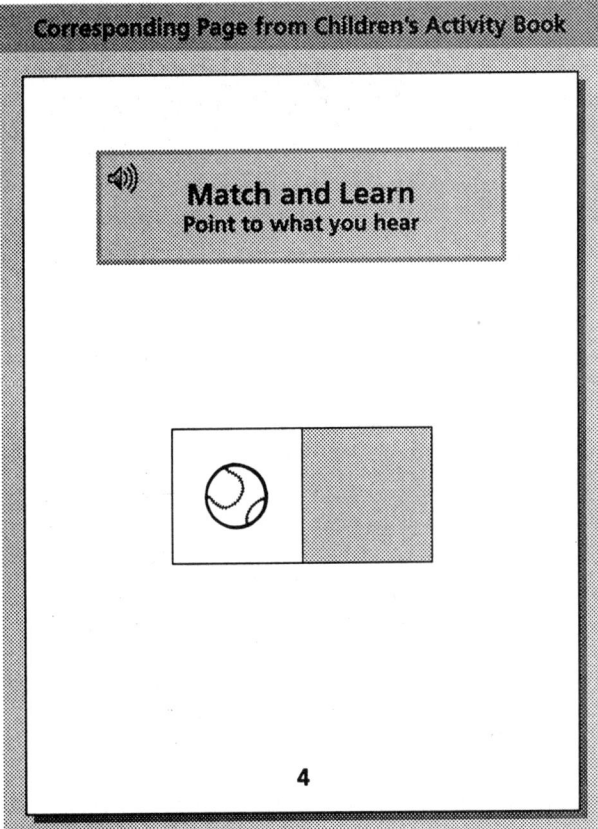

Ball... Of course, since the other box is empty, you point to the ball.

Match and Learn

This activity builds on the previous one, continuing the introduction to match and learn picture frames.

Instructions for This Page

Have your children look at the pictures in the frames in their activity books and point to the appropriate objects as directed by the tape.

Audio Transcript

Narrator: There are two frames, or sets of boxes, on this page. The top frame has two boxes with the number 1 to the left of them. In frame 1 you have two choices. You have to choose between two pictures. Listen and point to the picture of the word you hear. Remember we're only looking at the two boxes in frame 1 right now.

In frame one, point to the *Suppe*. Did you point to the soup? Good! *Suppe* is the German word for soup. And what is the other picture of? A ball? That's right! Do you remember the German word for ball? It's easy, isn't it? It's just *Ball*. Say it out loud, *Ball*. Good job.

Now look at the boxes in frame 2 and point to what you hear. *Stein*. You know it's not the *Suppe*, the soup, so it must be the rock, right? Good job. The German word for "rock" is *Stein*.

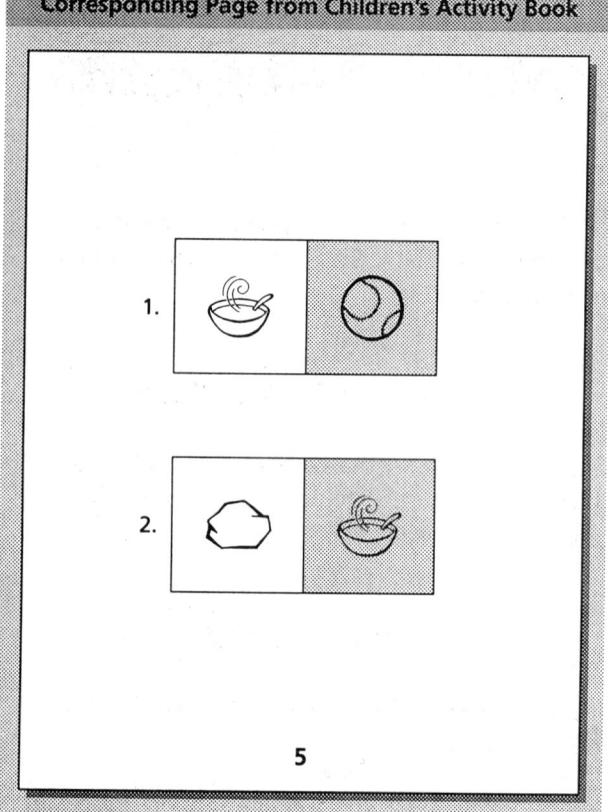

Corresponding Page from Children's Activity Book

Match and Learn

This activity builds on the previous one, continuing the introduction to match and learn picture frames.

Instructions for This Page

Have your children look at the pictures in the frame in their activity books and point to the appropriate objects as directed by the tape.

Audio Transcript

Narrator: Here is another frame. Point to what you hear.

Stein... Did you choose the rock? Good! But what is the other picture? Is it a *Ball*? That's right!

Now even with only these few words I can tell you a short story using some German. See if you can understand it.

Once upon a time a child was playing outside with a *Ball*. The child's mother said, "The *Suppe* is ready, come inside!" "Okay, mom, but I can't find my *Ball*. Can you help me find my *Ball*?" The mother went to help her child find the *Ball*, and she found it behind a great big *Stein*. Then they both went inside and ate *Suppe*.

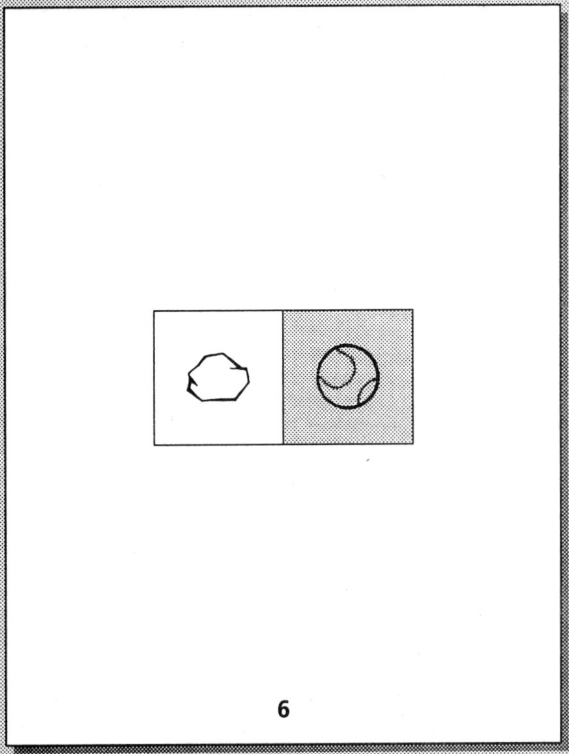

A Little Puzzle

This activity uses a puzzle to help your children become more familiar with the vocabulary words they learned in the previous activity.

Instructions for This Page

Have your children listen to the tape and point to the objects as the tape directs.

 Encourage your children to make sentences and comments much like the Narrator does, using the German vocabulary in the puzzle.

Audio Transcript

 Narrator: Now that you're familiar with frames, let's try a little puzzle. Listen and point to the words you hear.

First, point to the *Suppe*. It's in the top white box, right? Good! Now point to the *Ball*. It's in the bottom gray box, right? Yes. Now point to the *Stein*. The *Stein* is in the top gray box, right? Good work.

Now point to the *Schuh*. The what? The *Schuh*. You don't know what a *Schuh* is? You know what a *Stein* is, right? And you know what *Suppe* is, right? And you know what a *Ball* is, right? Well, there is only one other picture in the boxes. The shoe? Yes, the *Schuh*. Point to the *Schuh*. It's in the bottom white box, right? Yes.

That was easy.

A Girl and a Rat

Although it is important for children to first understand spoken language, it is exciting when they begin to use it, and that is where the learning really takes off. In this and the following activities we continue with comprehension building, but as the activity progresses, we gradually introduce conversation.

Your children will hear a simple story about a girl and a rat several times. They will learn the character names and identify them with pictures. By the time we get to them telling the story, they will have learned to recognize the pictures well enough that they can tell the story simply by looking at them. This builds fluency because they not only go beyond simple comprehension to actual production, but they think in German as they tell the story.

You'll notice that the story is told with a minimum number of words, and in very short, incomplete sentences (Girl sees rat. Rat sees girl., etc.). We do this to simplify communication and pattern it after how children begin communicating in their first language. For example, children say "water" when they mean, "I'm thirsty, please give me water." The same idea holds true in this and other similar activities. We'll start with the most basic communication structure and build from there. Eventually, we'll teach language for more complete sentences.

Instructions for This Page

Have your children look at the illustration for the story "A Girl and a Rat" and listen to the introduction to the story on the tape.

 Make sure your children understand each new German word introduced in the story. For those children who can read and write, teach them to spell each German word.

Corresponding Page from Children's Activity Book

Audio Transcript

Narrator 2: Activity: A Girl and a Rat.

Narrator: Now that you know a few German words, and have learned about frames, I can tell you a story—*Eine Geschichte*. I'll tell it to you with some English *Wörter* (words) *und* some German *Wörter*. I'll put in *Deutsche Wörter* only when you can easily guess what those *Wörter* mean.

My *Geschichte* is very short...*sehr Kurz*. It's about a little girl, *ein Mädchen*, and a rat, *eine Ratte*. Even though *meine Geschichte ist sehr Kurz*--very short, you can learn something about life from this *Geschichte*.

Figure out why *das Mädchen* in the *Geschichte* laughs, but *die Ratte* cries. I call *meine* little *Geschichte* "A Girl and a Rat." *Auf Deutsch* I call it "*Ein Mädchen und eine Ratte.*"

Match and Learn

This activity is visual, audio, and kinesthetic. It is designed to help your children learn by listening and pointing.

Instructions for This Page

Have your children point to the correct boxes and pictures as directed by the tape. In the second part of the activity, have them answer out loud the questions asked about the numbered pictures.

Audio Transcript

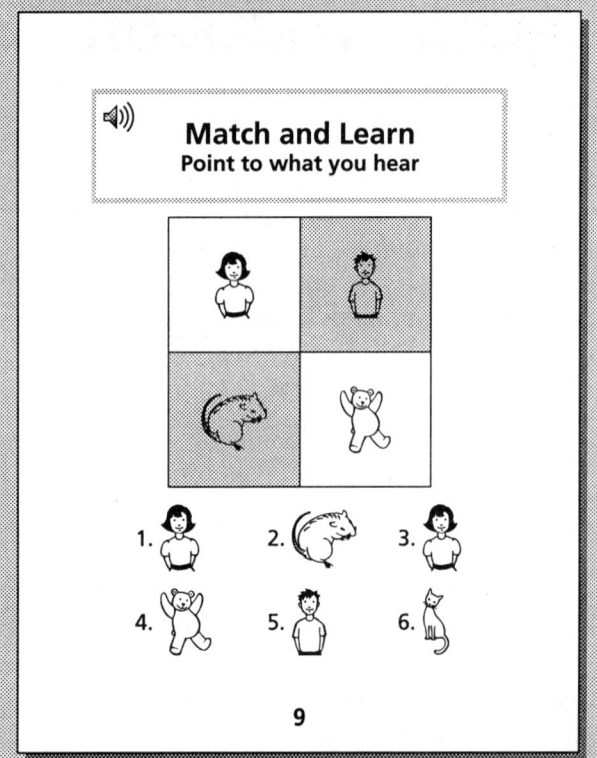

Corresponding Page from Children's Activity Book

 Narrator: Before I tell you the *Geschichte*, I'll teach you some new words to help you understand. Look at the frame with the white and shaded boxes.

Point to the girl, *das Mädchen*. *Das Mädchen* is in the top white box, right? Yes. Now point to *die Ratte*. *Die Ratte* is in the bottom shaded box, right? Now point to the bear, *der Bär*. Is *der Bär* in the top shaded box? No, *der Bär* is in the bottom white box, right? Now point to the boy, *der Junge*. He is in the top shaded box, right? Good.

Now, see if you can answer some questions about the words you just learned. Look at the picture with the number one next to it.

Number 1. Is this *ein Mädchen*? ... Yes, it is.

Number 2. Is this *eine Ratte*? ... Yes, it is.

Number 3. Is this *ein Mädchen* or *ein Junge*? ... Did you say *ein Mädchen*? Yes, it is a girl, it is *ein Mädchen*.

Number 4. Is this *ein Mädchen* or *ein Bär*? This is a bear, *ein Bär*.

Number 5. Is this *ein Junge*? ... Yes, this is a boy, *ein Junge*.

Number 6. Is this *eine Ratte*? ... No, this isn't a rat, this is a cat! Good.

Match and Learn

This activity uses the system of frames and numbered pictures learned in the previous activity. A few new German words are introduced.

Instructions for This Page

Have your children point to the correct pictures as the tape instructs. In the second part of the activity, they should answer out loud the questions asked about the numbered pictures.

 As these activities become progressively more challenging, the main objective is to help your children feel confident. They should not be overly concerned with correctness. Encourage them to point boldly as soon as they hear what to point to in the first part of the activity, and to speak out loud in response to the questions in the second half. When your children guess wrong, let them know it's okay and to keep making their best guesses.

Audio Transcript

 Narrator: You did very well with those pictures and words. Let's try a few more. Look at the frame with the white and gray boxes.

Point to *der Junge*. *Der Junge* is in the top gray box, right? Yes. Now, point to the cat, *die Katze*. Is *die Katze* in the top white box? Yes, *die Katze*, the cat, is in the top white box. Point to the tiger, *der Tiger*. *Der Tiger* is in the bottom white box, right? Now, point to *die Ratte*. *Die Ratte* is in the bottom gray box, right? Yes.

Now, see if you can answer some questions about the words you just learned. Look at the picture with the number one next to it.

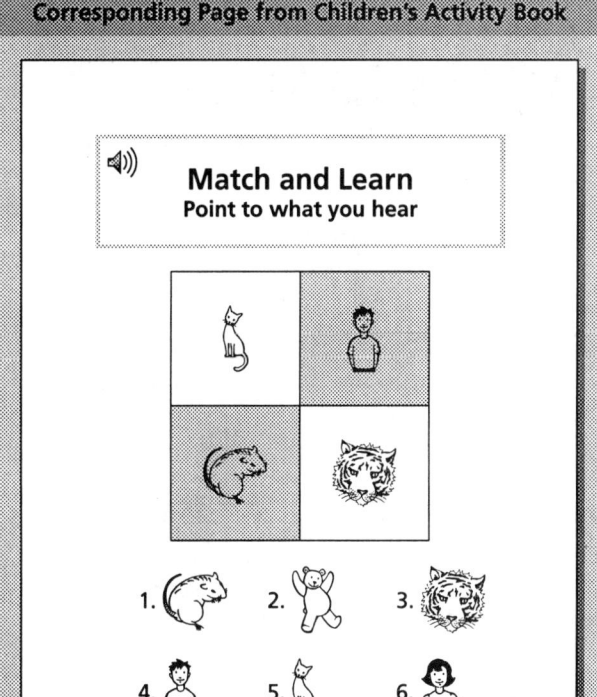

Number 1. Is this *eine Katze* or *eine Ratte*? It is *eine Ratte*.

Number 2. Is this *ein Mädchen* or *ein Bär*? This is *ein Bär*, a bear.

Number 3. Is this *ein Tiger*? Yes, it is.

Number 4. Is this *eine Katze* or *ein Junge*? This is *ein Junge*.

Number 5. Is this *eine Ratte*? No, it is not *eine Ratte*. It is *eine Katze*, right?

Number 6. Is this *ein Junge* or *ein Mädchen*? It's not a boy. It is *ein Mädchen*.

Diglot Weave

This activity contains a simple bilingual or diglot weave narrative built around two of the characters from the previous activities. This type of narrative was originally introduced by Professor Rudy Lentulay of Bryn Mawr University as a language learning aid.

Instructions for This Page

Have your children listen carefully and follow the story in their activity books as it is told on the tape.

 Have your children follow the words and pictures of the story with their finger, so that when the tape says the German word for "girl," for instance, their finger is pointing to the picture of the girl. This kinesthetic connection will enhance their mental connections between the German words and the ideas they represent. Once they feel comfortable with this diglot weave, have your children come up with a diglot weave of their own.

Audio Transcript

 Narrator: Now listen as I tell *die Geschichte* about *ein Mädchen und eine Ratte*. Follow along and look at the pictures.

Ein Mädchen sees *eine Ratte*. *Die Ratte* sees *das Mädchen*. *Die Ratte* squeaks "eek!" *Das Mädchen* squeaks back "eek!" *Die Ratte* runs. *Das Mädchen* chases *die Ratte*, but *die Ratte* escapes. *Das Mädchen* sits down *und* laughs "hee-hee-hee." *Die Ratte* sits down *und* cries "boo-hoo."

Did you like *meine Geschichte*? Did you understand all the words? I'll tell *die Geschichte* one more time and then ask you some questions about it.

Corresponding Page from Children's Activity Book

Diglot Weave
Ein Mädchen und Eine Ratte

Ein 👧 sees *eine* 🐭. *Die* 🐭 sees *das* 👧. *Die* 🐭 squeaks "eek!" *Das* 👧 squeaks back "eek!" *Die* 🐭 runs. *Das* 👧 chases *die* 🐭, but *die* 🐭 escapes. *Das* 👧 sits down *und* laughs "hee-hee-hee." *Die* 🐭 sits down *und* cries "boo-hoo."

11

Ein Mädchen sees *eine Ratte*. *Die Ratte* sees *das Mädchen*. *Die Ratte* squeaks "eek!" *Das Mädchen* squeaks back "eek!" *Die Ratte* runs. *Das Mädchen* chases *die Ratte*, but *die Ratte* escapes. *Das Mädchen* sits down *und* laughs "hee-hee-hee." *Die Ratte* sits down *und* cries "boo-hoo."

Now, I'll ask you some questions. Say your answers out loud. Did *das Mädchen* see a bear, *ein Bär*? No. Did *ein Bär* see *eine Ratte*? No! Did *die Ratte* see *ein Mädchen*? Yes! Did *die Ratte* run? Yes. Did *das Mädchen* chase *die Ratte*? Yes. Did *die Ratte* laugh? No. Did *das Mädchen* cry? No.

Match and Learn

This activity uses frames to introduce new pictures in the story. This time there are two pictures in each box instead of one, thereby increasing the difficulty of the activity.

Instructions for This Page

Have your children point to the correct pictures as the tape instructs.

Audio Transcript

 Narrator: Before I tell this *Geschichte* again, I'll teach you some more words and pictures.

Look at frame 1. Point to the box with the girl and the running legs. Did you point to the top white box? Good. The running legs mean "runs." Together, the pictures in this box mean "girl runs." Now, point to the box with only the girl. The girl is in the bottom gray box. Point to "rat runs." "Rat runs" is in the top gray box. Now point to "boy runs." Did you point to the bottom white box? Good.

Now, look at frame 2. Point to *die Ratte*. *Die Ratte* is in the top gray box, right? Now, point to "bear roars." "Bear roars" is in the top white box. See the two pictures: the bear and the roar? This means "bear roars." Point to "rat runs." Did you point to the bottom gray box? Good. Now point to "rat squeaks." "Rat squeaks" is in the bottom white box. Do you see the two pictures: the rat and the eek? This means "rat squeaks."

Let's look now at frame 3. Point to "girl squeaks." Did you point to the top white box? Good. Now, point to "bear roars." "Bear roars" is in the bottom white box. Point to "rat runs." Did you point to the top gray box? Good. Now, point to "girl runs." "Girl runs" is in the bottom gray box, right?

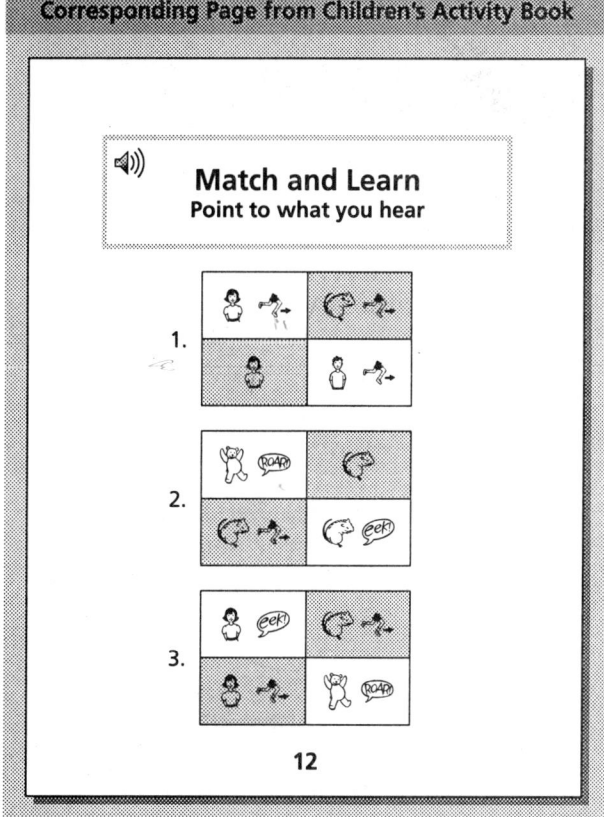

Corresponding Page from Children's Activity Book

Match and Learn

This activity uses frames once again to introduce more new pictures that can be incorporated into the telling of the story. And once again, this activity is slightly more challenging than the previous one because it contains some boxes with as many as three pictures to identify.

Instructions for This Page

Have your children point to the correct pictures as the tape instructs.

Audio Transcript

 Narrator: Now let's learn the German words for the pictures you just learned.

Look at frame 4. Point to "girl sees rat." "Girl sees rat" is in the top white box. See the three pictures: the girl, the eye, and the rat? Together, the pictures in this box mean "girl sees rat." In German it would be, *Mädchen sieht Ratte*. Now, point to "rat runs," or *Ratte läuft*. *Ratte läuft* is in the bottom gray box, right? Point to "*Ratte sieht Mädchen.*" Did you point to the top gray box? Good. Now, point to *Mädchen jagt*, or "girl chases." "*Mädchen jagt*" is in the bottom white box, right? Good.

Now, look at frame 5. Point to *Ratte jagt Mädchen*, "rat chases girl." "Rat chases girl" is in the top white box, right? Now, point to "rat squeaks," or *Ratte piepst*. Did you point to the bottom white box? Good. Point to *Ratte sieht*. *Ratte sieht* is in the top gray box. Now, point to *Mädchen läuft*. Did you point to the bottom gray box? Good.

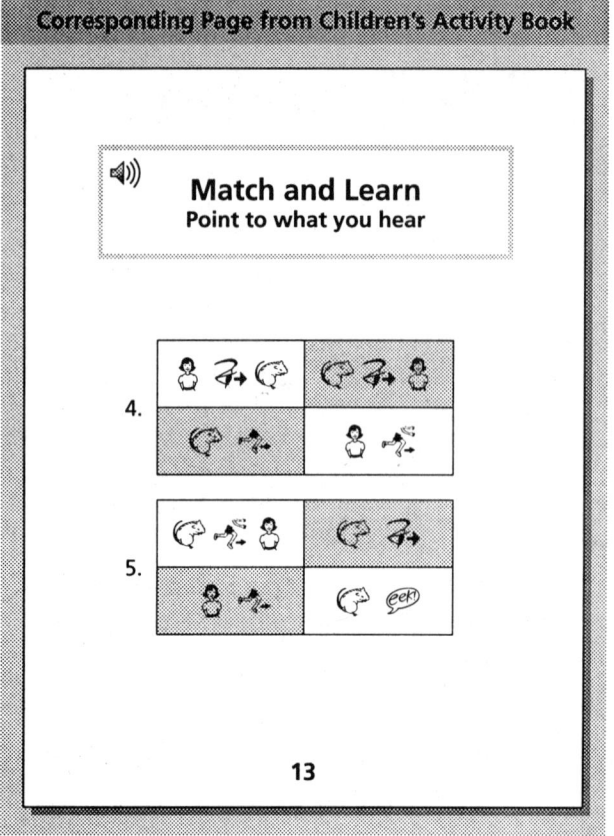

Rebus Story

This activity is designed to help your children begin to think in German. This is accomplished by having pictures in their activity books represent the German words read on the tape. This way your children will associate the German words with their English equivalents.

Instructions for This Page

Have your children follow the pictures with their finger as the German words for those pictures are read on the tape.

 This is a good activity for drawing pictures and creating flashcards. Encourage your children to create stories of their own!

Audio Transcript

Narrator: Now that you know the story, try to follow the pictures as I tell you the story all in German. There are a couple of new words at the end. See if you can figure out what they mean. Are you ready? Good! Here we go!

Mädchen sieht Ratte. Ratte sieht Mädchen. Ratte piepst. Mädchen piepst. Ratte läuft. Mädchen jagt. Ratte entkommt. Mädchen lacht. Ratte weint.

Were you able to follow along? Could you tell that *entkommt* means to escape, and that *lacht* means to laugh and *weint* means to cry? Good!

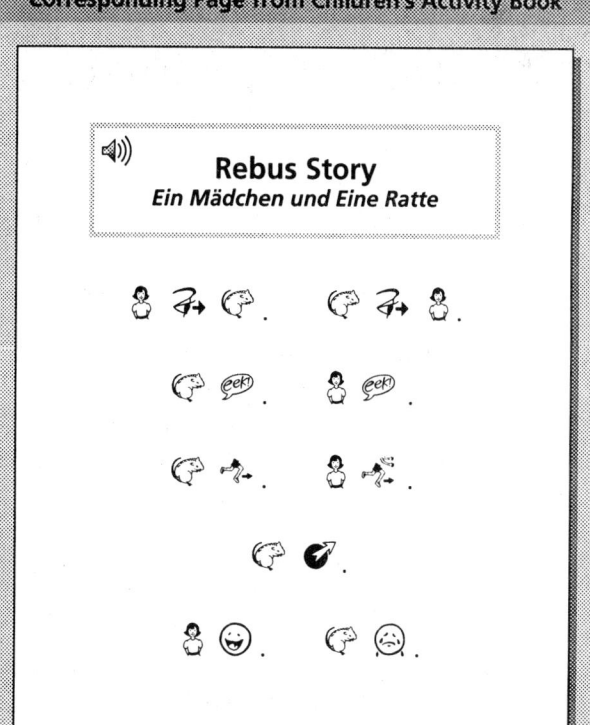

Describe What You See

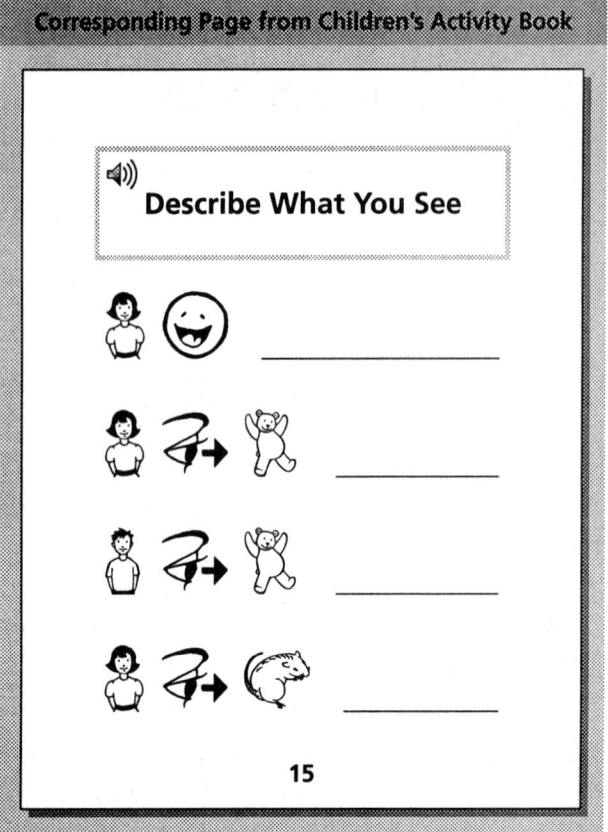

This activity requires your children to use the German words they learned in the previous activity to describe the pictures they see.

Instructions for This Page

Have your children say the German words for the pictures, or write them on the blank lines to the side of the pictures.

Have your children say or write in as many of the German words as they can on their own. Then you may go back through with them and help them remember those they missed. Continue to encourage them to guess when they need to, and to not feel bad when they cannot remember all the words or when they get one wrong.

Audio Transcript

Narrator: On this page are some of the pictures you have learned the words for. Say the German words for the pictures. Or if you like, write the German words for the pictures in the blanks.

Story Telling

This activity lets your children use the German words they have learned to tell the story of "A Girl and a Rat" themselves.

Instructions for This Page

Have your children follow the trail of pictures (from top to bottom) with their finger, telling the story using the German words for the pictured items as they go.

If your children cannot remember a particular word, let them think for a moment, and then go ahead and help them. Your goal here is to encourage them to think as hard as they can on their own, while keeping them from getting frustrated or discouraged. Encourage them to create their own stories using the pictures in this activity.

Audio Transcript

 Narrator: Follow the trail of pictures from top to bottom with your finger, telling the story using the German words for the pictures.

Practice in German

The following activity begins with the story of "A Girl and a Rat" read entirely in German.

This activity then asks your children to tell the story entirely in German on their own, using the pictures in the circle below the German text as memory prompts.

Instructions for This Page

First have your children follow the German text in their activity books as it is read on the tape.

Then have them cover the German text, look at the pictures in the circle below the text, and try to tell the story in German on their own. Record how long it takes them to tell the complete story in German their first time, and then record their best subsequent time.

 Let your children try telling the story as many as six or eight times, perhaps even looking back at the German text on the top of the page and learning the German articles and other connecting words found there. Have them rearrange the sentences, thereby creating their own story.

Audio Transcript

 Narrator: Last of all, here is *die Geschichte* all in perfect *Deutsch*. Listen carefully.

Ein Mädchen sieht eine Ratte. Die Ratte sieht das Mädchen. Die Ratte piepst--eek! Das Mädchen piepst--eek! Die Ratte läuft. Das Mädchen jagt die Ratte. Aber die Ratte entkommt. Das Mädchen lacht--hee-hee-hee! Die Ratte weint--boo-hoo!

Were you able to follow along and understand? Good!

Corresponding Page from Children's Activity Book

Practice in German
Listen carefully, then tell the story

Ein Mädchen sieht eine Ratte. Die Ratte sieht das Mädchen. Die Ratte piepst--eek! Das Mädchen piepst--eek! Die Ratte läuft. Das Mädchen jagt die Ratte. Aber die Ratte entkommt. Das Mädchen lacht--hee-hee-hee! Die Ratte weint--boo-hoo!

First Time

Fastest Time

17

A Treasure Map

This section contains an audio transcript of the adventure story your children will hear on the tape.

Instructions for This Page

Have your children listen carefully as the adventure story is read on the tape. Encourage your children to take an active part in listening to the adventure story. Ask them to respond to things they hear and have them say out loud words said by the characters on the tape.

Younger children might enjoy coloring the picture as the adventure story is read. Older children may want to follow along with the written audio transcript provided in this *Parent's Guide*.

Audio Transcript

 Narrator 2: The Adventure Continues: A Treasure Map

Narrator: After Dieter finishes telling you the story of the Girl and the Rat, you say, "That was cool listening to your story in German, Dieter. I did kind of know some of the words already, and it was fun learning the new words using pictures."

Max: Yeah, it was. So the first clue is Build on what you know. Got it!

Dieter: Very good, Max. Just remember the clues as you go along, and you'll find the treasure in the end. And it is a magnificent treasure indeed!

Narrator: "It sounds exciting!" you say. "And maybe before we go to bed tonight we should also learn the words for the shapes on this map, so we can ask people how to find the places."

Dieter: That's an excellent idea. I'll teach you the German words for lines and shapes, and I'll introduce you to a few numbers while we're at it. How does that sound?

Serena: It sounds fun, Dieter!

Max: Yeah.

Lines and Figures

The following activity is a learning game that uses pictures to help your children learn some new words. The activity is deliberately simple in order to help your children develop confidence in their ability to comprehend a foreign language.

Instructions for This Page

Have your children look at the pictures in their activity books and point to the shapes as they hear the words for those shapes read on the tape. The narrator will read each word twice in German, then go back through the words in German one by one, and finally read the German words all together.

 Help your children identify the right shapes during the first part of the activity (when each new word is read twice). Then let them try pointing on their own after that.

Have your children pause the tape as needed to have time to give their answers.

Audio Transcript

 Narrator 2: Activity: Lines and Figures.

Narrator: Here on your activity book page are the things Dieter teaches you about.

Point to what you hear. Circle...*Kreis, Kreis.* Square...*Quadrat, Quadrat.* Line...*Linie, Linie.* Triangle...*Dreieck, Dreieck.*

Did you point to them all? Good job! Now let's go through them once more, in German only.

Point to what you hear.

Dreieck, Quadrat, Kreis, Linie. Did you point to them all? Good job!

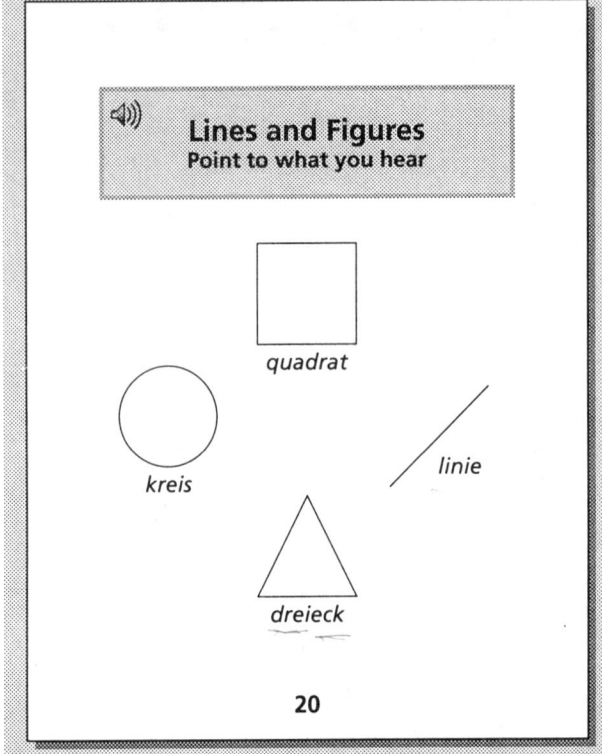

Look and Listen

This activity uses the shapes from the previous page in several different combinations.

Learning to identify more than one of the same shape (two circles or three lines, for instance) and various shapes grouped together will give your children added confidence.

Instructions for This Page

Have your children look at the numbered pictures of shapes and sets of shapes in their activity books as the words for those shapes are read on the tape.

 Encourage your children to point to each shape with their finger and count when appropriate as the words are read on the tape. For example, on number 12 they could point to the two squares one by one immediately after *"zwei Quadrate"* is read on the tape, then point to the line as *"und eine Linie"* is read on the tape.

Audio Transcript

 Narrator: On this page, point to what you hear.

Number 1. *Kreis*...circle. *Ein Kreis.*

Number 2. *Quadrat*...square. *Ein Quadrat.*

Number 3. *Dreieck*...triangle. *Ein Dreieck.*

Number 4. *Linie*...line. *Eine Linie.*

Number 5. *Ein Dreieck und ein Quadrat.* One triangle and one square.

Number 6. *Ein Kreis und ein Dreieck.* One circle and one triangle.

Number 7. *Zwei Kreise.* Two circles.

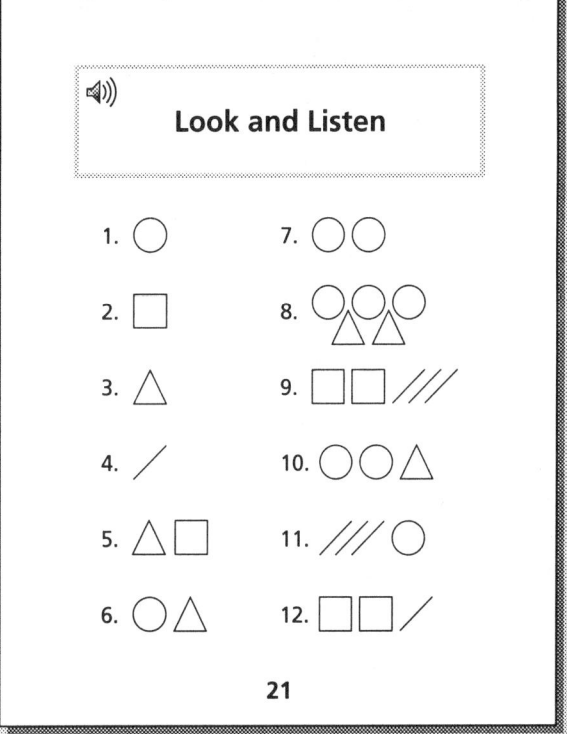

Corresponding Page from Children's Activity Book

Number 8. *Drei Kreise und zwei Dreiecke.* Three circles and two triangles.

Number 9. *Zwei Quadrate und drei Linien.* Two squares and three lines.

Number 10. *Zwei Kreise und ein Dreieck.* Two circles and one triangle.

Number 11. *Drei Linien und ein Kreis.* Three lines and one circle.

Number 12. *Zwei Quadrate und eine Linie.* Two squares and one line.

Well done.

Point to What You Hear

This time the shapes will be read in German only. This activity builds the same identification skills as the previous activity, and also reviews the basic German numbers.

Instructions for This Page

As before, have your children look at the pictures in their activity books and point to the shapes and sets of shapes as they hear the German numbers and words for those shapes read on the tape. Then encourage them to call out the German words before they are read on the tape.

Audio Transcript

 Narrator: Now look and listen again. This time I'll say just the German names of the shapes, and I'll mix up the order. You point to the shapes that you hear. Ready? OK.

Point to *zwei Kreise*. It's number 7, right?

Now point to *ein Dreieck*. It's number 3, right?

Now point to *zwei Quadrate und eine Linie*. It's number 12, right?

Now point to *zwei Quadrate und Drei Linien*. It's number 9, right?

Now point to *eine Linie*. It's number 4, right?

Now point to *ein Kreis*. It's number 1, right?

Now point to *ein Dreieck und ein Quadrat*. It's number 5, right?

Now point to *Drei Linien und ein Kreis*. It's number 11, right?

Now point to *ein Quadrat*. It's number 2, right?

Now point to *Drei Kreise und zwei Dreiecke*. It's number 8, right?

Now point to *ein Kreis und ein Dreieck*. It's number 6, right?

And last of all, point to *zwei Kreise und ein Dreieck*. It's number 10, isn't it?

Were you able to point to most of them? Very well done.

Match and Learn

This activity is visual, audio, and kinesthetic. It is designed to help your children learn by listening and pointing.

Instructions for This Page

Have your children look at the pictures in each numbered frame in their activity books and point to the box which contains the shapes whose names are read on the tape. All of frame one will be read; thereafter, the names for the shapes in three of the four boxes will be read before the tape goes on to the next frame. This will allow for a process of elimination to take place as your children go through the boxes in each numbered frame.

If it's helpful or fun, encourage your children to mark off the boxes already selected as they go along.

Audio Transcript

Narrator: Now let's do some match and learn activities. Point to what you hear.

Look at frame 1. Point to *ein Kreis*. It's in the bottom white box, right? Good. Now point to *zwei Dreiecke*. It's in the top white box, right? Now point to *ein Dreieck*. It's the bottom gray box. Now point to *zwei Kreise*. It's the top gray box, right?

Now look at frame 2. Point to the box with *zwei Kreise*. It's the top gray box, right? Now point to *zwei Dreiecke*. It's the bottom gray box. Now point to *zwei Linien*. It's the top white box, right?

Now look at frame 3. Point to the *Quadrat*. It's the top white box, right? Now point to *zwei Quadrate*. It's the top gray box, isn't it? Now point to *eine Linie*. It's the bottom white box, right? Well done!

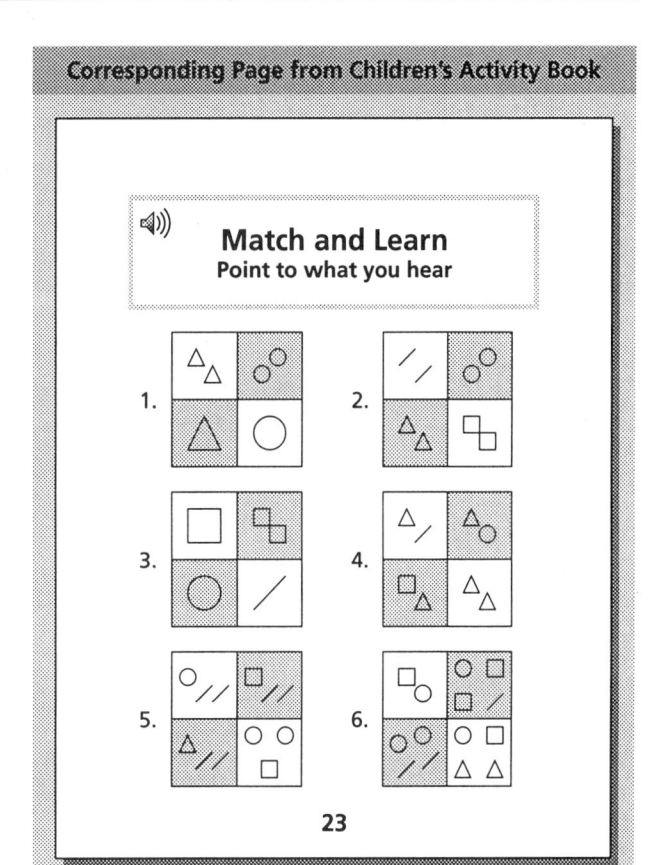

Now look at frame 4. Point to *zwei Dreiecke*. It's the bottom white box, right? Now point to *ein Quadrat und ein Dreieck*. It's the bottom gray box, right? Now point to *ein Dreieck und eine Linie*. It's the top white box, right?

Now look at frame 5. Point to *zwei Linien und ein Dreieck*. It's the bottom gray box. Now point to *zwei Kreise und ein Quadrat*. It's the bottom white box. Now point to *zwei Linien und ein Quadrat*. It's the top gray box, right? Yes.

Now look at frame 6. Point to *ein Kreis, zwei Dreiecke und ein Quadrat*. It's the bottom white box, isn't it? Now point to *ein Kreis, zwei Quadrat und eine Linie*. It's the top gray box. Now point to *ein Quadrat und ein Kreis*. It's the top white box, right? Well done.

Lines and Figures — Match and Learn

Listen and Draw

After your children develop their ability to comprehend, they'll begin to produce. This activity reinforces their ability to comprehend by having your children do something kinesthetic and creative: drawing what is heard. Drawing helps your children internalize what is being learned because they will have to interpret what is heard in a creative form.

Instructions for This Page

Have your children listen to the descriptions of sets of shapes read on the tape and draw what they hear. These will be combinations of multiple numbers of the same shapes and various other shapes (for instance, number 1 calls for "Two lines and one circle"). Have your children draw all of the shapes for each number in the gray "chalkboard" box next to that number.

Have your children pause the tape as needed to have time to give their answers.

Audio Transcript

Narrator: These chalkboards are for you to draw on. You'll be drawing squares, *Quadrate*; circles, *Kreise*; triangles, *Dreiecke*; and lines, *Linien*.

I'll name the shapes and you draw them. You can turn off the tape while you get something to write with if you need to. Are you ready? OK. Here we go.

Number 1. *Zwei Linien und ein Kreis. Zwei Linien und ein Kreis.* Two lines and one circle.

Number 2. *Zwei Kreise und eine Linie. Zwei Kreise und eine Linie.* Two circles and one line.

Number 3. *Eine Linie, ein Quadrat, ein Kreis, und ein Dreieck. Eine Linie, ein Quadrat, ein Kreis, und ein Dreieck.* One line, one square, one circle, and one triangle.

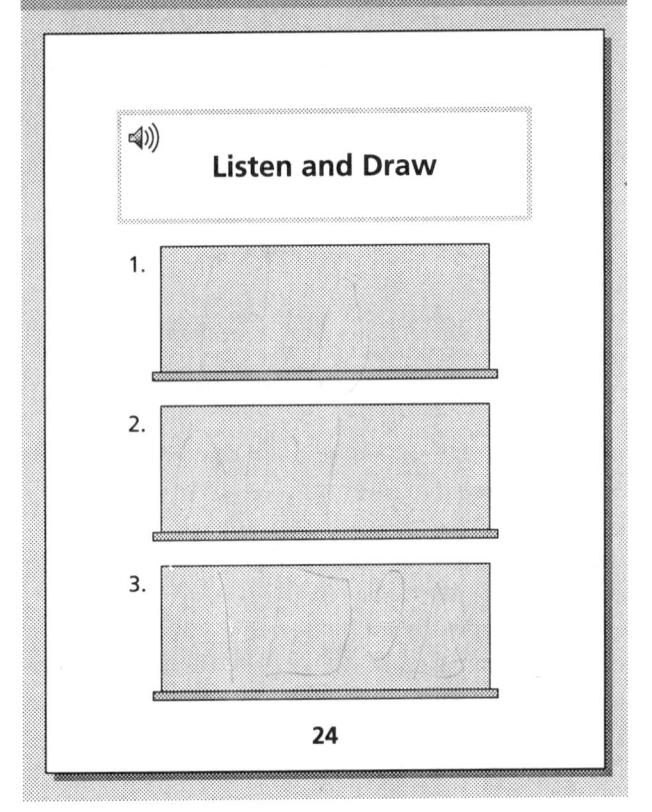

Power-Glide **Children's German**

Listen and Draw

Here are the chalkboards with the correct shapes drawn on them.

Instructions for This Page

Compare these drawings to those of your children. Point out the similarities and the differences. Be sure to compliment your children on what they drew correctly.

After reviewing your children's drawings, have them look at the sample "answer" drawings in their activity books as the corresponding German words are read again on the tape.

Audio Transcript

Narrator: Here are the same chalkboards, but with my drawings on them. Do your drawings look something like mine? Let's look at each chalkboard together.

Number 1. *Zwei Linien und ein Kreis.*

Number 2. *Zwei Kreise und eine Linie.*

Number 3. *Eine Linie, ein Quadrat, ein Kreis, und ein Dreieck.* This is a full chalkboard, isn't it?

Corresponding Page from Children's Activity Book

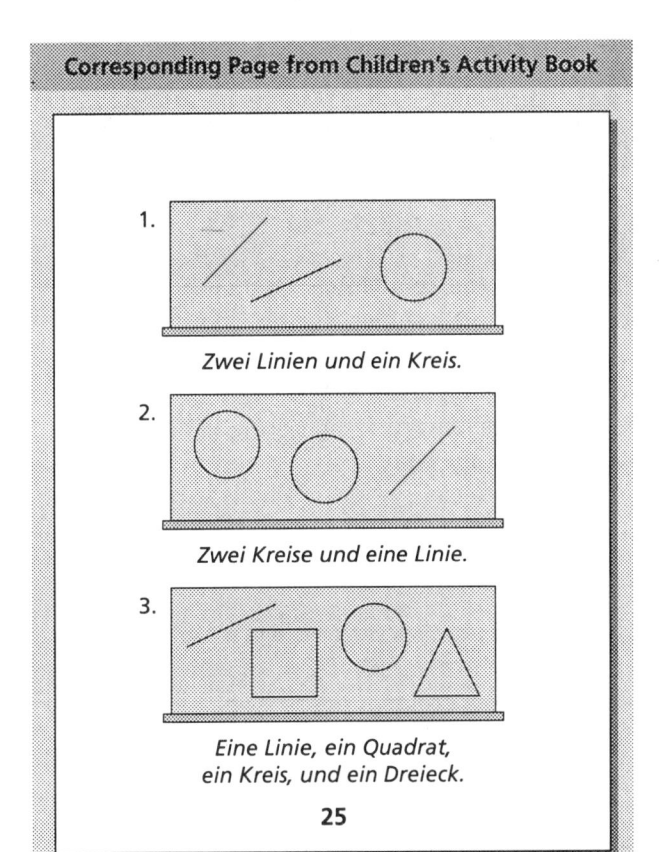

1. *Zwei Linien und ein Kreis.*

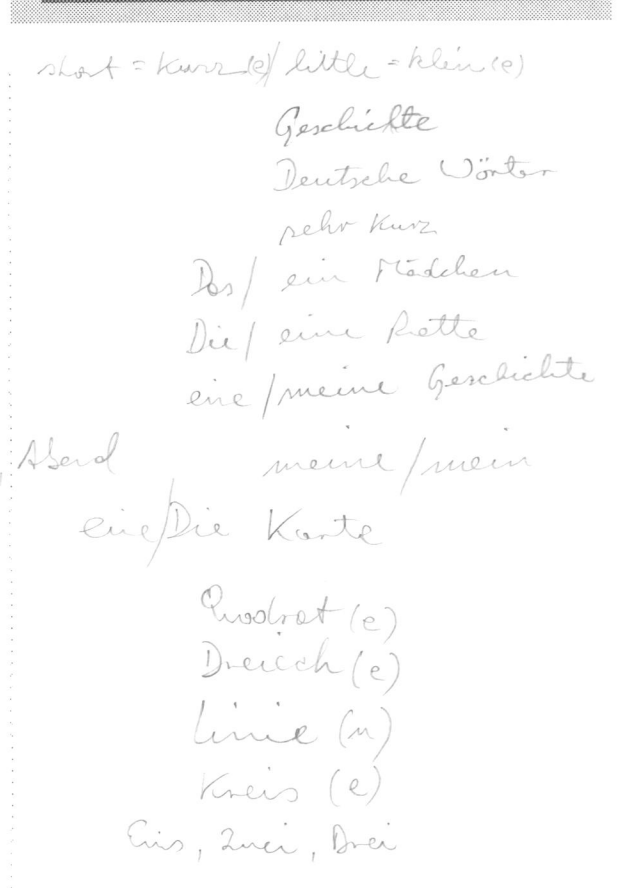

2. *Zwei Kreise und eine Linie.*

3. *Eine Linie, ein Quadrat, ein Kreis, und ein Dreieck.*

25

Lines and Figures — P–33 — Listen and Draw

Look and Say

This activity lets your children verbalize the words they have been hearing on the tape. And since they have to say the German words based solely on looking at the shapes (rather than just reading German words), it also tests their actual knowledge of the words.

Instructions for This Page

Have your children point to the first four shapes and tell you the names of the shapes in German. Next have your children describe what is drawn on each chalkboard.

Encourage your children to use both German shape names and German numbers in describing the contents of the chalkboards.

Have your children pause the tape as needed to have time to give their answers.

Have your children come up with their own order of shapes and draw them on new "chalkboards." This will encourage them to internalize the language and develop their own creativity.

Audio Transcript

Narrator: Look at the shapes on your activity book page. As you point to each shape, say what its name is in German.

Number 1. It's *ein Kreis*. Did you say *ein Kreis*? That's right.

Number 2. *Ein Quadrat.*

Number 3. *Ein Dreieck.*

Number 4. *Eine Linie.*

Now chalkboards. Say what you see on each of the chalkboards.

Corresponding Page from Children's Activity Book

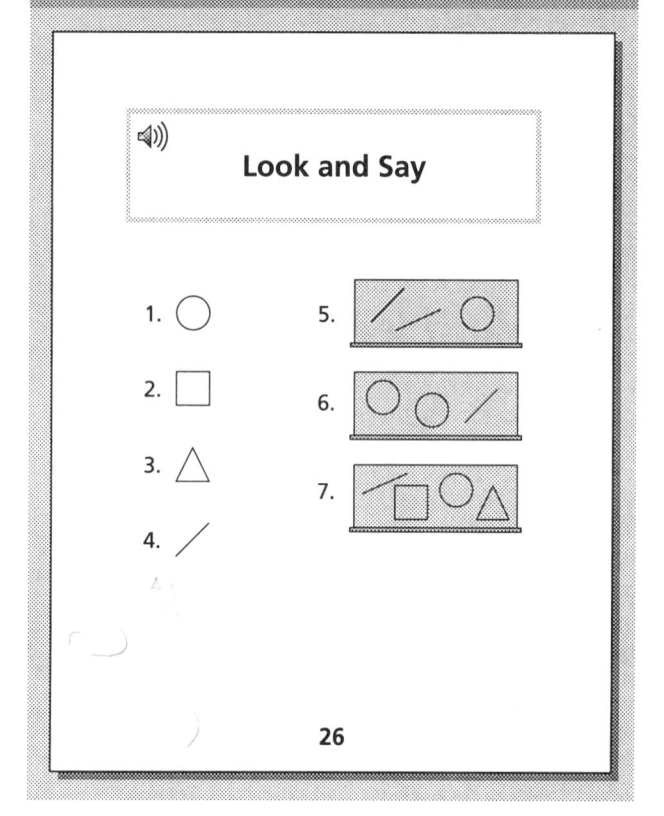

Look and Say

1. ○
2. □
3. △
4. ╱
5. ╱ ○
6. ○ ○ ╱
7. □ ○ △

26

Number 5. *Zwei Linien und ein Kreis.*

Number 6. *Zwei Kreise und eine Linie.*

Number 7. *Eine Linie, ein Quadrat, ein Kreis und ein Dreieck.*

Meeting Heidi at the Market

This section contains an audio transcript of the adventure story your children will hear on the tape.

Instructions for This Page

Have your children listen carefully as the adventure story is read on the tape. Encourage your children to take an active part in listening to the adventure story. Ask them to respond to things they hear and have them say out loud words said by the characters on the tape.

Younger children might enjoy coloring the picture as the adventure story is read. Older children may want to follow along with the written audio transcript provided in this *Parent's Guide*.

When your children get to the part of the adventure story where Heidi makes *Kartoffelsalat* and *Wienerschnitzel*, stop the tape and turn to the Recipes section at the back of this *Parent's Guide* to find the recipes. Try making some!

Audio Transcript

Narrator 2: The Adventure Continues: Meeting Heidi at the Market

Narrator: As you finish that activity, Max yawns long but quietly.

Max: <yawning> Uh! I'm really tired. How about you guys?

Serena: So am I.

Narrator: "Me too," you agree, yawning yourself.

Nicole: Alright. It is bedtime for all of us, I think. There is only one room on this floor of the house, I'm afraid, but I thought you three might like to sleep up in the loft anyway. It's got a window that looks right out over the river and the water wheel, and there are four warm beds up there, so even with three of you that leaves one. I have some extra pajamas that my nieces and nephews use when they come to visit, and that will give the clothes you have on now a chance to completely dry, too.

Max: That sounds perfect, Nicole.

Serena: Lots better than sleeping in the forest, especially!

Dieter: Good! Well, I'll see you all at breakfast.

Narrator: Without any more encouragement you, Serena and Max all climb up the ladder into the cozy loft, get into dry clothes and go to bed. You are all asleep in no time, and don't wake up until the sun is already shining brightly through the big loft window the next morning. Downstairs you can hear Nicole singing as she and Dieter work the mill. The you, Max and Serena sleepily climb down out of the loft and find Nicole waiting for you.

Nicole: Ah, *Guten Morgen*, my friends!

Continued from Children's Activity Book, page 27

Serena: *Guten Morgen!*

Max: *Guten Morgen!*

Nicole: *Wie geht's euch?*

Narrator: "I feel great this morning," you say.

Serena: Yeah, I'm a bit sore from all that paddling and swimming we did, but I'm excited to explore the valley.

Max: Yeah, and I'll be glad to talk to my parents and let them know we're OK.

Nicole: Yes, you should go into the village and call them on the radio right away. I can give you a quick breakfast before you go.

Serena: Thanks a lot, Nicole. And could you teach us that song you were singing, too? I heard the words *Guten Morgen,* and some of the rest sounded familiar too, but I didn't understand all of it.

Nicole: Certainly, I'll teach it to you while you eat. In English it goes:

<TUNE: "Are You Sleeping">

> Good morning, Good morning!
> Miss Hut, Miss Hut!
> How are you today?
> How are you today?
> Thanks, good. Thanks, good.

And in German it's:

> *Guten Morgen, Guten Morgen!*
> *Fräulein Hut, Fräulein Hut!*
> *Wie geht es Ihnen heute?*
> *Wie geht es Ihnen heute?*
> *Danke, gut. Danke, gut.*

Max: That's a great song, Nicole!

Nicole: Do you really like it? I'm glad. Let's sing it all together, then.

Narrator: "OK," you agree, and you join in with Nicole, Serena and Max.

Nicole, Max, Serena:

> *Guten Morgen, Guten Morgen!*
> *Fräulein Hut, Fräulein Hut!*
> *Wie geht es Ihnen heute?*
> *Wie geht es Ihnen heute?*
> *Danke, gut. Danke, gut.*

Nicole: *Wunderbar,* my friends! You are very quick learners. I'm impressed.

Serena: *Danke,* Nicole!

Nicole: Now then, you really had better be on your way into the village. There will be many people out looking for you by now, worrying and risking their lives. Follow the way marked on your map, and you should get to the radio office in only half an hour. And after you have radioed Max's parents, you can look for the first X on your map. I think you'll find it in the middle of the market, very near the radio office. Good luck!

Narrator: You, Serena and Max take off down the winding road through the jungle to the village. In the trees all around you strange birds and other animals call to each other in harsh, eerie voices, and the sun is almost completely shut out by the over-arching canopy of leaves and branches high above you. Every now and then you see wild animals crossing the road or scurrying into the bushes far ahead of you, and when you turn and look back the way you have come you sometimes see large eyes staring back at you out of the bushes you have just passed.

After a half hour or so of good hiking you come out of the jungle into the outskirts of the village. Well kept houses line the streets, and it isn't hard at all to find the center of town. Right next to the market, just as Nicole said, is the radio office. The three of you go inside and with the help of a friendly radio operator, soon have Max's father on the radio.

Dad: Max! Are your cousins with you? Are you okay?

Max: Yeah, Dad. They're right here, and we're all fine. We tried to follow my lizard using your raft, but the current in the river swept us down into a big valley. Everyone here speaks German.

Continued from Children's Activity Book, page 27

Dad: Yes, I know about the valley. That's good! I'll charter a plane and come pick you up right away. I should be able to get there in just a couple of hours. By the way, your lizard came back home on his own. He's here now.

Max: Oh, good. I was worried about him. But dad, do we really have to come home so soon?

Dad: What's the matter?

Max: Well, we've heard that this valley has some special treasures. I wish we could stay long enough to find out more about them.

Dad: Treasures, huh? It sounds like you and your cousins have found yourselves quite an adventure.

Max: That's not even the best part!

Serena: We're learning German!

Dad: Well, now, that's a wonderful adventure indeed! But I'm worried. Do you have any place to stay?

Max: Yes. Last night we stayed with a young couple named Nicole and Dieter, they run a mill on the river. They invited us to stay with them until the regular plane comes through again.

Dad: Are you sure it's no problem for them to have you stay for a few days? I wouldn't want to impose on anyone.

Narrator: "I don't think so," you say. "Nicole said it was just fine. She enjoyed having us there a lot."

Max: Please, Dad?

Dad: Well... Are you sure you and your cousins would rather spend the first week of their vacation in the valley, instead of here at our house?

Serena: Oh, yes! Could we?

Max: Please?

Dad: Well, OK! Your mother is nodding that it's fine with her, and with Nicole and Dieter looking out for you, I suppose it's fine with me too! Well, we'll see you in about a week, then! Call us again every day or so to let us know everything is all right, OK?

Max: No problem. Thanks, Dad!

Narrator: The three of you are very excited that you'll be able to spend your week treasure hunting in the valley, and you decide to go right away into the market and try to find the spot marked by the first X on your map.

Serena: Wow, look at how cool this market is, you guys.

Max: Yeah, I don't think I've ever seen lots of these fruits and vegetables before. They must be tropical things that only grow in really warm places like this.

Narrator: "It is cool to be in a real open air market," you say. "And I'm hungry, too. Let's get some lunch here."

Max: Good idea. But before we eat, though, I want to find where the first X is. Who has the map?

Serena: I do. It's right here.

Max: Hmmm. It looks like the first X is over there somewhere ... Maybe near that big food stand with all the sodas stacked in front. Let's go over and ask that girl working at the stand. The one who's humming to herself.

Narrator: The three of you approach the big food stand and introduce yourselves.

Serena: *Guten Tag! Ich heiße* Serena.

Max: And *Ich heiße* Max.

Narrator: You tell the girl your name as well and she says.

Heidi: *Es ist nett Dich kennenzulernen. Ich heiße* Heidi.

Narrator: "It's nice to meet you, Heidi," you say in English. But what does "*Es ist nett Dich kennenzulernen*" mean?

Heidi: <laughing> It means just what you said—"It's nice to meet you." And you say you're looking for a *Schatz*, a treasure?

Max: Yes. Can you help us?

Continued from Children's Activity Book, page 27

Heidi: Yes, I think I can. The next spot on your map, your *Karte,* is right here. I have the next piece of your treasure myself. If you would like to join me for some lunch, and then help me prepare some of the food I sell here at my stand, I'll give it to you.

Serena: Mmmm. That sounds great. We were just saying how hungry we are, and it will be fun to learn how to make some more German foods! Last night Nicole taught us to make dumplings.

Heidi: *Wunderbar.* First then, let's all have some lunch.

Narrator: The four of you sit around a shaded table near Heidi's stand and enjoy a delicious lunch. As you eat, she tells you about the valley you are exploring and also about her homeland of Austria. "Cool, Heidi!" you say. "You're from Austria?"

Heidi: *Ja.* It is a wonderful place. You would love it.

Serena: Tell us about Austria, Heidi! Are Austrians Germans?

Heidi: Actually, no. Austria is it's own country, separate from Germany, and most Austrians don't like being called Germans. Austria has a distinct culture and history of its own. Austria is especially famous for its great musicians, such as Haydn, Mozart, Schubert, Strauss, Beethoven and Brahms. Austrians love music, and they love the outdoors, too—especially winter sports. Austrians are known for their relaxed and happy approach to life, their *Gemütlichkeit,* as it is called. They love good food a lot, and make many different kinds of food that are popular in the cultures all around them. My recipes are examples.

Max: That's really neat, Heidi. I think it would be really cool to visit Austria. I was also wondering, what was that song you were humming to yourself as we walked up to your stand earlier? I couldn't understand the words.

Heidi: Oh, that? That was just a little song I made up about some of the food I sell. In English it goes:

<TUNE: "Ten Little Indians">

Bread, milk, butter cheese,
Fat, ice cream, fruits and veggies,
Fish, meat, eggs, noodles,
These are my foods.

And in German it goes:

Brot, Milch, Butter, Käse,
Fett, Eis, Früchte, Gemüse,
Fisch, Fleisch, Eier, Nudeln,
Das sind meine Speisen.

Serena: That's a fun song, Heidi! Can you teach it to us?

Heidi: *Natürlich!* Here is the first line again: Bread, milk, butter cheese. In German it's *Brot, Milch, Butter, Käse.* Let's sing that together…

Heidi, Serena, Max: *Brot, Milch, Butter, Käse.*

Heidi: And the second line is: Fat, ice cream, fruits and veggies. *Fett, Eis, Früchte, Gemüse.* All together again…

Heidi, Max, Serena: *Fett, Eis, Früchte, Gemüse.*

Heidi: Good! Now: Fish, meat, eggs, noodles. *Fisch, Fleisch, Eier, Nudeln.*

Heidi, Max, Serena: *Fisch, Fleisch, Eier, Nudeln.*

Heidi: And last of all, These are my foods. *Das sind meine Speisen.*

Heidi, Max, Serena: *Das sind meine Speisen.*

Heidi: Very good! Now let's sing the whole song once more all together.

Heidi, Max, Serena:

Brot, Milch, Butter, Käse,
Fett, Eis, Früchte, Gemüse,
Fisch, Fleisch, Eier, Nudeln,
Das sind meine Speisen.

Heidi: *Wunderbar,* my friends. You learned that song quite easily. And now, I think, it's time for us to begin cooking. I need to prepare some more potato salad—*Kartoffelsalat,* and some more *Wienerschnitzel.*

Continued from Children's Activity Book, page 27

Serena: Those sound delicious. Let's get started making them!

Heidi: They are both quite delicious, *sehr lecker.* Here, you can work here, Serena; and Max, you stand right here…

Narrator: Heidi shows you, Serena and Max each what to do, and you spend a fun afternoon helping her prepare the foods she will sell at dinner time. As you work, you say, "Wow. There are so many colorful things here at the market."

Max: Yeah. I can see things of almost every color in the rainbow. I wish I knew the German words for all the colors.

Serena: Me too.

Heidi: How about I teach you while we prepare these recipes. I can use these sodas right here to start with. All the different flavors are different colors!

Colors at the Market

This activity introduces the German words for basic colors: white, black, red, green, yellow, blue, orange, brown, purple and pink.

In this activity, your children are asked to color soda bottles in the different colors in order to help them connect the German words with the various colors. Once the bottles are colored, your children are asked to point to the colors (in German) which they hear on the tape. This reinforces the German color names in their minds.

Instructions for This Page

Have your children use crayons, markers or colored pencils to color in the bottles as the tape directs them. The two bottles in the top row are already colored white and black. Once the bottles are all colored, have your children point to each colored bottle as the tape directs them.

💡 Since color words in the second half of the activity are reviewed by color rather than by bottle order or number. The order in which your children color the bottles is not important. Simply help them point to the correct colored bottles as the German color words are read. The tape will help them check themselves as well. As ever, try to help your children guess boldly and not worry if they are occasionally wrong.

Audio Transcript

🔊 Narrator 2: Activity: Colors at the Market.

Narrator: The bottles on your activity book page are like the ones you see at the market, only the ones on your page aren't colored yet.

To make your bottles look like the ones you see Heidi's market stand, take out some crayons or markers or colored pencils. You will need these colors, these *Farben*: red, green, yellow, blue, orange, black, brown, purple, pink, and white. A box of sixteen crayons or markers should have all of those. You may stop the tape if you need to go get some.

Have you got something now to color with? Good! Let's begin. As I say the English and German words for a color, pick any one of the empty white bottles on your activity book page and color it in with that color. Stop the tape as often as you need to in order to have time to color. Are you ready? OK. Here we go.

The first soda Heidi points to is a strawberry flavor. It's bright red! So, pick one of the bottles on your page, and color it bright red! Are you finished? Good! The German word for red is *rot*. That's easy to remember, isn't it? Say it out loud: *rot*.

The next bottle is a bottle of milk. It is all white. Color one of your bottles white. Heidi points to a bottle of milk and says: *weiß*. Say it out loud: *weiß*. That means "white" in German.

Continued from Children's Activity Book, page 28

The next bottle Heidi points to has black cherry flavored soda in it. It is black. Color one of your bottles black. The German word for "black" is *schwarz*. Say it out loud: *schwarz*.

The next flavor of soda Heidi points to is lime. It is a delicious looking green color. Pick one of your bottles, and color it green. Are you finished? Good! The German word for green is *grün*. Can you remember that? Say it out loud: *grün*.

After that, Heidi points to a lemon flavored soda. It is colored yellow, *gelb*. Say it out loud: *gelb*. Now color one of your bottles *gelb*. Are you finished coloring one of the bottles yellow? Good.

Next Heidi points to a blue colored soda. It is some kind of fruit punch. She tells you that the German word for blue is *blau*. Say it out loud: *blau*. So, pick another bottle and color it *blau*—color it blue. Are you finished? Good.

The next bottle Heidi points to has orange flavor soda in it. Can you guess what color it is? That's right! It is orange! That was too easy! The German word for orange is *orange*. That one is really easy, isn't it! Pick another empty bottle and color it *orange*. Are you finished? Good.

After showing you the orange soda, Heidi points to a cola drink. It is brown. Pick one of your bottles and color it brown. Are you finished? Good! The German word for brown is *braun*. Can you say that? *Braun. Braun.*

The second to last soda Heidi points to is grape flavored—purple. she tells you the German word for purple is *lila*. So, pick one of the bottles you haven't colored yet, and color it *lila*—purple. Are you finished? Good.

The last soda bottle is full of pink lemonade. Heidi points to it and says: *rosa*. *Rosa* means pink! That one is easy to remember because it sounds like a rose, and lots of roses are pink. So, color the last bottle *rosa*. Are you finished? Excellent!

Well, you should have all the bottles colored in now. That's a lot of colors to learn, isn't it? You aren't sure you'll ever be able to remember them, but Heidi helps you. She says the German words for the colors and lets you point to the soda you think it is. Let's do the same thing together. I'll say a color in German, and you try to point to the right colored soda bottle on your activity book page. Ready? OK, here goes.

Grün. Point to the soda you colored *grün*. Did you point to the green soda? Good! Now another.

Blau. Point to the soda you colored *blau*. Did you point to the blue soda? Good. Now another.

Gelb. Point to the soda you colored *gelb*. Did you point to the yellow soda? That's right. Now another.

Rot. Point to the soda you colored *rot*. Did you point to the red soda? Well done. Now another.

Rosa. Point to the soda you colored *rosa*. Did you point to the pink soda? Good. Now another.

Braun. Point to the soda you colored *braun*. Did you point to the brown soda? Right again. Now another.

Orange. Point to the soda you colored *orange*. Did you point to the orange soda? Good. Now one more.

Lila. Point to the soda you colored *lila*. Did you point to the purple soda? Well done.

Scatter Chart

This activity continues to teach German colors by having your children identify and color fruits, vegetables and other things at the market that are the different colors they have learned.

Instructions for This Page

As colors are said on the tape, have your children use crayons, markers or colored pencils to color in the appropriate item.

Audio Transcript

Narrator: Once she has taught you the colors at the soda stand, Heidi takes you around the market, telling you colors and asking you to find things that are those colors. For example, she starts by asking you to find something that is *weiß*, something that is white. You only have to look for a minute to find a man selling milk. Milk is *weiß*!

So let's practice. As I say a color in German, find one of the pictures on your activity book page that is of something which is usually that color. Are you ready? OK. Find something on this page that is usually *gelb*. Did you pick the banana? Good! Bananas are usually *gelb*, aren't they? Go ahead and color the banana *gelb*—yellow. Are you finished coloring the banana *gelb*? Good. Now let's try another color.

Try to find something on this page that is usually *grün*. Can you see anything that is usually *grün*? I see something—the lettuce! Lettuce is usually *grün*, isn't it? So, go ahead and color the lettuce *grün*—green. Are you finished coloring? Good.

Now look at your page and see if there is anything on it that is usually *rot*. What do you think? Is it the cherries? I'd say so! Cherries are usually very *rot*. So, go ahead and color the cherries *rot*. Are they colored *rot* now? Good job.

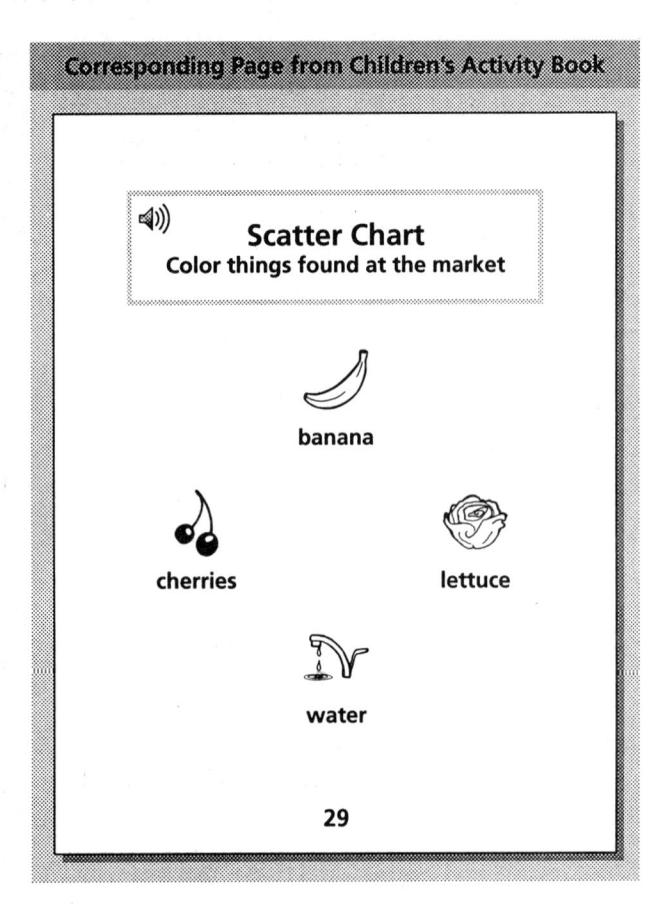

The last thing on your page is some water. Can you guess what color water is, like in the ocean, or in a lake? That's right! It's blue—*blau*! So, color the water *blau*—color it blue. Are you finished? Good.

Corresponding Page from Children's Activity Book

Scatter Chart
Color things found at the market

banana

cherries   lettuce

water

29

Match and Learn

This activity tests your children on the four colors reviewed in the previous activity. Your children are asked to point to the correct items based solely on their color names in German.

Instructions for This Page

Have your children point to the items in the various frames that are the colors said on the tape. For instance, when the tape says to point to the item in frame 1 that is *gelb*—yellow, your children should point to the box in that frame which is yellow—the banana.

Have your children pause the tape as needed to have time to give their answers.

Audio Transcript

Narrator: Now that you've learned a few of the German words for colors, let's see which ones you can remember. As I say a color in German, point to the thing in your activity book which is that color. For example, when I say point to something that is *grün*, you point to the lettuce, because it is green. Are you ready? OK, here goes.

Look at the large frame on your activity book page. Point to the thing that is *rot*. Did you point to the cherries? Good! That's right! A cherry is *rot*—it is red! Now point to the thing that is *gelb*. Did you point to the banana? Well done! The banana is *gelb*—yellow. Now point to the thing that is *blau*. Did you choose the water? Good! The water is blue—*blau!*

Now look at the numbered shapes at the bottom of your page. As I say what each thing is, say out loud what color it is in German!

Here we go:

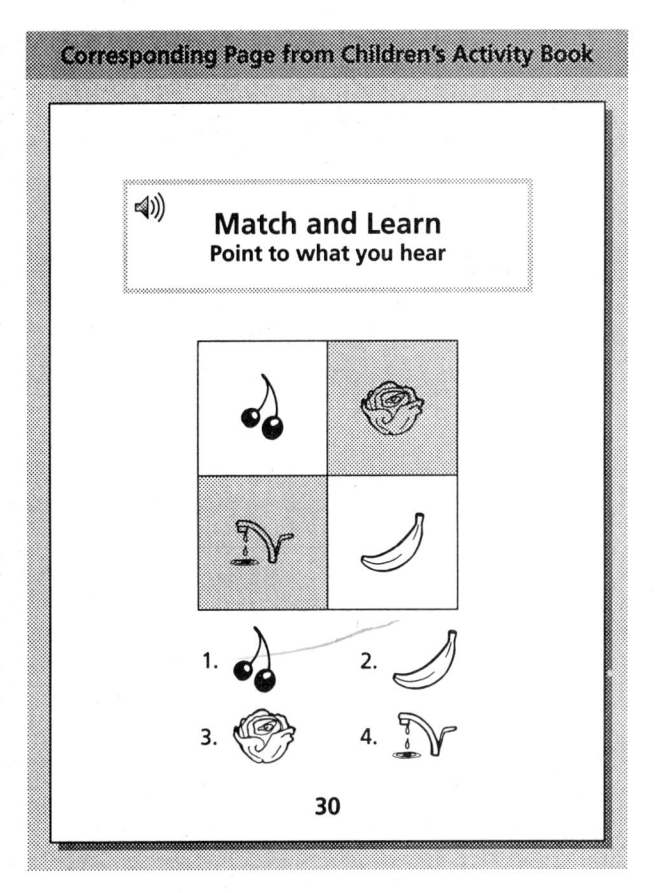

Number 1: A couple of cherries. Did you say *rot*? That's right! Cherries are *rot*!

Number 2: A banana. Did you say *gelb*? Yes, bananas are *gelb*.

Number 3: A head of lettuce. Did you say *grün*? Good.

Number 4: Water. Did you say *blau*? Good.

Scatter Chart

This activity continues to teach German colors by having your children identify and color fruits, vegetables and other things at the market that are the different colors they have learned.

Instructions for This Page

As a color is said on the tape, have your children use crayons, markers or colored pencils to color in the appropriate item.

Audio Transcript

Narrator: You did a great job remembering those colors. Now let's try to find things that are some other colors.

The next color Heidi asks you to find is *lila*. Can you see something on your page that is often *lila*—often purple? The grapes? Right! You look around the market and find some purple grapes. There are other grapes that are *grün*, but the ones you pick are *lila*. So, take out your colors, and make the grapes purple! Are you finished? Good!

The next color Heidi asks you to find is *braun*—something that is *braun* color. See if you can find something on your page that is usually *braun*. Did you pick the potato? Nice work! Potatoes are usually *braun* color, aren't they? They are usually brown. So, color the potato on your page *braun*.

Next, Heidi asks you to look for something *orange*. See if you can find something on your page that is usually *orange*. Is a carrot usually *orange*? Yes, a carrot usually is *orange*—it usually is orange! So, color the carrot on your page *orange*.

The last thing on your page is a rose. Do you remember the German word for pink? That's right! It's *rosa*. Heidi asks you to find something at the market that is *rosa*, and you find a beautiful rose. It is the pinkest thing you've ever seen! So, color the rose on your page *rosa*.

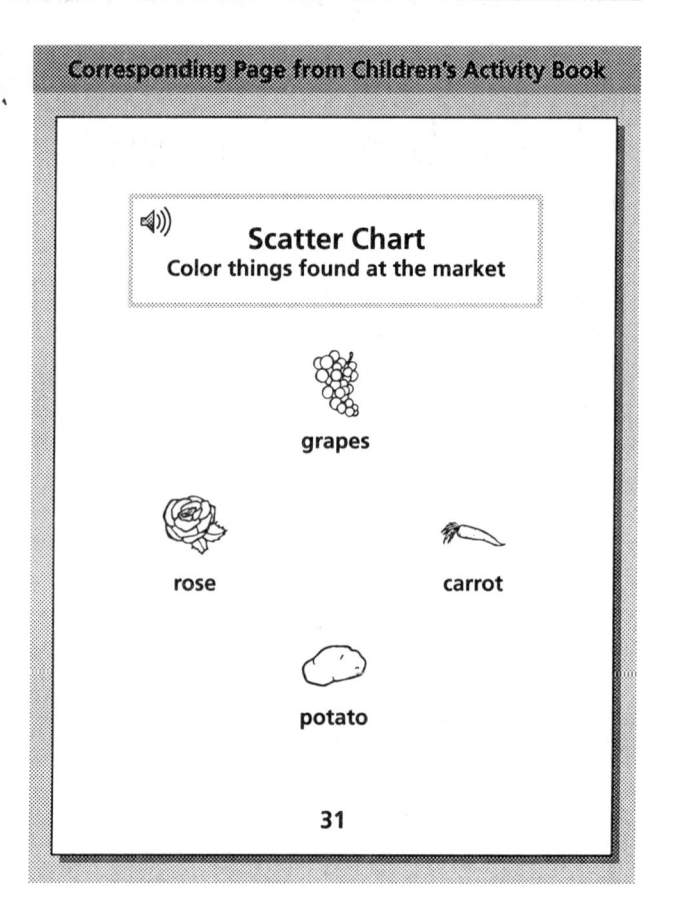

Corresponding Page from Children's Activity Book

Scatter Chart
Color things found at the market

grapes

rose   carrot

potato

31

Match and Learn

This activity tests your children on the four colors reviewed in the previous activity. Your children are asked to point to the correct items based solely on their color names in German.

Instructions for This Page

Have your children point to the items in the various frames that are the colors said on the tape. For instance, when the tape says to point to the item in frame 1 that is *braun*—brown, your children should point to the box in that frame which is brown—the potato.

Have your children pause the tape as needed to have time to give their answers.

Audio Transcript

Narrator: Now that you've learned a few more of the German words for colors, let's see which ones you can remember. As I say a color in German, point to the thing in your activity book which is that color. For example, when I say point to something that is *braun*, you would point to the potato, because it is brown—*braun*. Are you ready? OK, here goes.

Look at the large frame on your activity book page. Point to the thing that is *lila*. Did you point to the grapes? Good! That's right! Grapes are *lila* in color—they are purple! Now point to the thing that is *orange*. Did you point to the carrot? Well done! Carrots are *orange* color, aren't they? Now point to the thing that is *rosa*. Did you choose the rose? Good! The rose is pink, *rosa*!

Now look at the numbered shapes at the bottom of your page. As I say what each thing is, say out loud what color it is in German!

Here we go:

Corresponding Page from Children's Activity Book

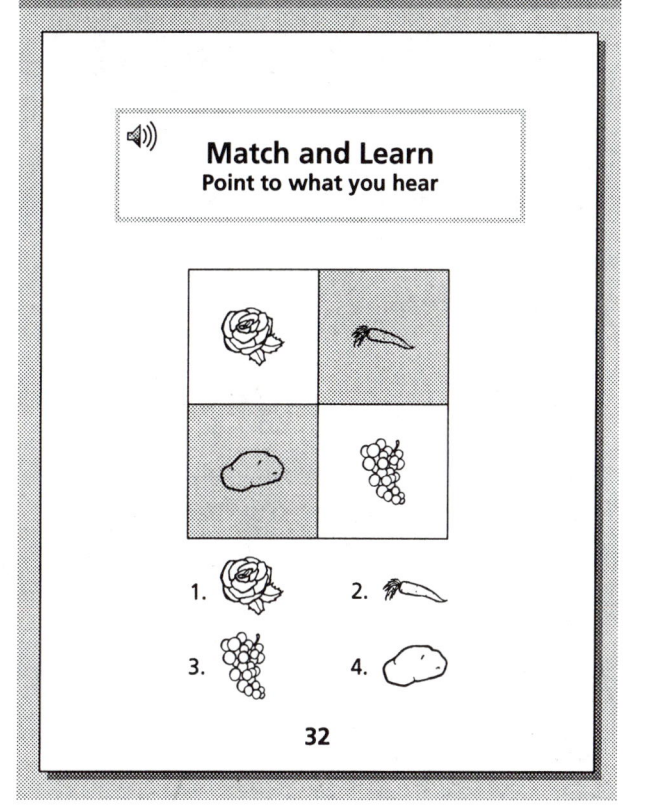

Match and Learn
Point to what you hear

Number 1: A rose. Did you say *rosa*? That's right! A rose is *rosa*—it is pink.

Number 2: A carrot. Did you say *orange*? That's right! A carrot is *orange*.

Number 3: A bunch of grapes. Did you say *lila*? Good!

Number 4: A potato. Did you say *braun*? Good!

Colors at the Market — Match and Learn

Match and Learn

This activity tests your children on all of the colors learned in this activity. Your children are asked to point to the correct items based solely on their color names in German.

Instructions for This Page

Have your children point to the items in the various frames that are the colors said on the tape.

Audio Transcript

Narrator: Now that we've reviewed the German words for all the colors, let's see which ones you can remember. As I say a color in German, point to the thing in your activity book which is that color. For this exercise, you will also need to remember the German words for black and white. The German word for "black," if you remember, is *schwarz*. The German word for "white" is *weiß*. *Schwarz* and *weiß*. Black and white. Now are you ready to review all the colors? Good! As I say the colors, point to the right item in each frame.

Look at frame 1. Point to the thing that is *lila*. Did you point to the grapes? Well done! Now point to the thing that is *weiß*. Did you point to the white bottle? Good job! Now point to the thing that is *gelb*. Did you choose the banana? Nice work. The last thing in this frame is a potato. Do you remember what color a potato is? That's right! It's *braun*—brown.

Now look at frame 2. Can you see something here that is *rot*? The cherries? Right! How about *orange*? Can you see anything here that is *orange*? The carrot? Correct! And finally, do you see anything *rosa* here? The rose? Exactly. The rose is *rosa*. Good memory!

Corresponding Page from Children's Activity Book

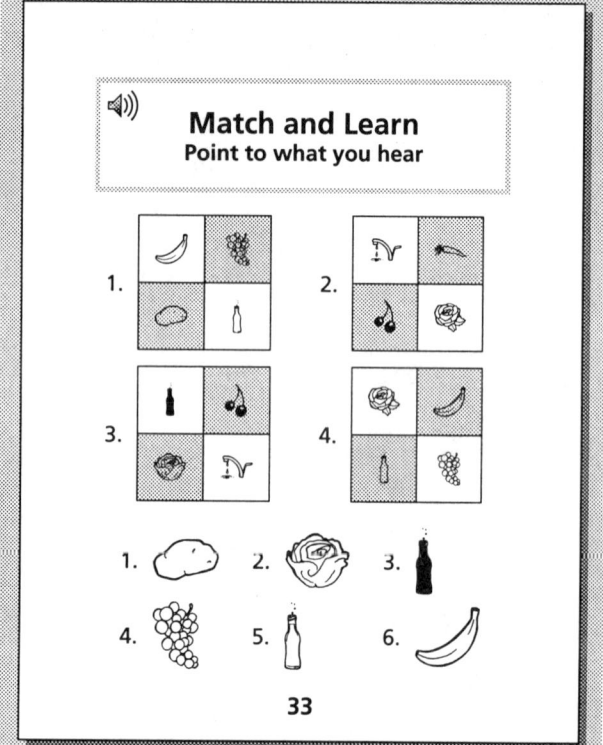

Match and Learn
Point to what you hear

1. 2.
3. 4.

1. 2. 3.
4. 5. 6.

33

Now look at frame 3. Which of these things is *blau*? Is it the lettuce? No, the lettuce is *grün*! The water is *blau*! Now, which thing is *rot*? The cherries? Right on! And which thing is *schwarz*? The bottle? That's right! And finally, which thing is *grün*? The lettuce? Of course! We just told you that! And you remembered anyway.

Now look at frame 4. Point to the thing that is *weiß*. Did you point to the white bottle? Well done! Now, point to the thing that is *gelb*. Did you choose the banana? Well done! And now, point to the thing that is *lila*. The grapes, right? You've learned these colors very well.

Now look at the numbered shapes at the bottom of your page. As I say what each thing is, say out loud what color it is in German!

Here we go:

Number 1: A potato. Did you say *braun*? That's right! A potato is *braun*—it is brown.

Number 2: A head of lettuce. Did you say *grün*? That's right!

Continued from Children's Activity Book, page 33

Number 3: A bottle of black cherry soda. Did you say *schwarz*? Excellent!

Number 4: A bunch of grapes. Did you say *lila*? Good!

Number 5: A bottle of milk. Did you say *weiß*? Well done!

Number 6: A banana. Did you say *gelb*? Perfect!

You've learned your colors very well.

Animals at the Zoo

This section contains an audio transcript of the adventure story your children will hear on the tape.

Instructions for This Page

Have your children listen carefully as the adventure story is read on the tape. Encourage your children to take an active part in listening to the adventure story. Ask them to respond to things they hear and have them say out loud words said by the characters on the tape.

Younger children might enjoy coloring the picture as the adventure story is read. Older children may want to follow along with the written audio transcript provided in this *Parent's Guide*.

Audio Transcript

Narrator 2: The Adventure Continues: Animals at the Zoo

Max: That was a fun way to learn colors, Heidi.

Narrator: "Yeah," you agree. "Learning new stuff is cool when you learn it in fun ways."

Heidi: That's true. And now that you mention it, I almost forgot to give you the piece of your *Schatz* you came here searching for. It is: Make learning fun.

Serena: Make learning fun. OK. That's easy to remember. *Danke*, Heidi.

Heidi: You're welcome. And thank you all very much, *danke schön,* for your help this afternoon. I could never have prepared so much food without the three of you.

Corresponding Page from Children's Activity Book

The Adventure Continues
Animals at the Zoo

Max: You're welcome, Heidi. It's been really fun. And maybe we'll see you again tomorrow. *Guten Nacht!*

Heidi: *Guten Nacht!*

Narrator: You, Max and Serena leave the market and begin the short walk back to Nicole and Dieter's house. The evening shadows are just beginning to fall as you arrive. After dinner you spend the evening talking with Nicole and Dieter, telling them about your adventures of the day.

Early the next morning you, Serena and Max set out toward the village again, looking for the second spot marked on your map. When you get to the village, you take out your map and look at it carefully.

Serena: Let's see, the next X looks like it's over that way, on the other side of this market. There's a little picture of a cage by it. I wonder what that is for?

Narrator: "Maybe," you say, "it means there's a jail nearby."

Continued from Children's Activity Book, page 35

Max: No, not a jail, a zoo! Look, there's a bear in the cage.

Serena: A zoo! I love zoos. Let's hurry!

Narrator: The three of you rush through the village, stopping briefly to say hi to Heidi as you go through the market, and in almost no time at all you reach the gates of a big zoo. "Wow," you say, "this looks like a big zoo. There must be lots of animals here."

Max: Yeah. Where should we start?

Serena: How about with the monkeys, over there?

Max: All right, let's go!

Narrator: The three of you walk from one area of the zoo to another for almost an hour, looking at tigers and elephants, snakes, monkeys and lizards. There's even a lizard like Max's, but a lot bigger.

Max: Cool! Look at that monster lizard! I bet that's what dinosaurs looked like.

Serena: I think it's creepy how his tongue goes in and out. Let's go on to the next display.

Narrator: "OK," you say. "And let's start looking around for the treasure that we're supposed to find here."

Max: Yeah, good idea. We haven't seen any sign of that.

Narrator: You, Serena and Max continue on, looking at one display after another, until you finally come to a big caged in wilderness area with a giant bear roaming around in it.

Serena: Look, you guys! It's a bear, just like the one shown in the picture of the cage on our map. Maybe this is it—the place we'll find our next piece of our treasure!

Narrator: Just as Serena says that, an old zoo keeper comes out from behind the enclosure wall to your left.

Wolfgang: So, you are looking for a treasure, a *Schatz*, are you?

Max: Uh, ya. I mean, *ja*. We are. We have a treasure map, a *Karte*, that has a big X marking a place somewhere here in the zoo, we think. Is that right?

Wolfgang: Yes, it is. *Ich heiße* Wolfgang. I am a keeper here at this zoo. *Wie heißt ihr?*

Max: *Ich heiße* Max.

Serena: *Ich heiße* Serena.

Narrator: You introduce yourself in German as well, and then Wolfgang says:

Wolfgang: You have found the right place. I have the next piece of your treasure, and if you'll help me take care of some of the animals here in the zoo today, I will give it to you.

Serena: You mean, you'll let us help you feed the animals and stuff?

Wolfgang: Yes. And I'll tell you a story or two as well.

Max: Cool!

Narrator: "Yeah," you say. "Cool."

Serena: I've never fed any big animals before. Won't they eat us up?

Max: Yeah, it sounds cool, but Serena is right—I think I'd be scared to feed a bear, for example. Isn't it dangerous?

Wolfgang: No, not if you know how to act when you're around them. Here, come with me, *kommt mit mir*, and I'll show you what to do.

Narrator: You all go with Wolfgang and he shows you around the places of the zoo where only the keepers go. It's really fun to see how everything works, and to get a closer look at some of the animals. As you go along, Wolfgang tells you a little bit about his home country of Luxembourg.

Wolfgang: I actually lived in Africa for several years before coming here, but I was born and I grew up in Luxembourg, a very small country found right in the middle of Germany, Belgium and France. Luxembourg's culture has been influenced by all three of those countries, and German is only one of Lux-

Continued from Children's Activity Book, page 35

embourg's three official languages. Hiking and cycling are two of the favorite sports in Luxembourg, and the people there tend to be less in a hurry than people in other European countries. Part of the famous Tour de France passes through Luxembourg. It's a small country, like I said, but people from there have a lot of national pride. And actually it's real full name is the Grand Duchy of Luxembourg.

Serena: The Grand Duchy of Luxembourg? Wow, that sounds really important. Thanks for telling us about it, Wolfgang. You're the first person from Luxembourg we've ever met!

Wolfgang: You're quite welcome, my friends.

Narrator: After helping Wolfgang for a while, you all take a break and he offers to tell you a story.

A Boy and a Bear

Although it is important for children to first understand language, it is exciting when they begin to use it, and that is where the learning really takes off. This activity moves in that direction. It is very close in format to the earlier, "A Girl and a Rat" activity.

Instructions for This Page

Have your children look at the first page of the story "A Boy and a Bear" and listen to the introduction to the story on the tape.

Audio Transcript

Narrator 2: Activity: A Boy and a Bear.

Narrator: Here is the story Wolfgang tells you. It is called *Ein Junge und Ein Bär:* A Boy and a Bear.

Match and Learn

This activity is visual, audio, and kinesthetic. It is designed to help your children learn by listening and pointing.

Instructions for This Page

Have your children point to the correct boxes and pictures as the tape instructs. In the second part of the activity, have them answer out loud the questions asked about the numbered pictures.

Have your children pause the tape as needed to have time to give their answers.

Audio Transcript

Narrator: You already know some of these words. Let's go over them. First, point to *die Ratte*. Did you point to the rat, in the top white box? Good. Now, point to *der Junge*, the boy. The *Junge* is in the top gray box, right? Next, point to the bear, the *Bär*. The *Bär* is in the top white box, right? No, the *Bär* is in the bottom gray box. Now, point to the *Mädchen*, the girl. The *Mädchen* is in the bottom white box, right? Good.

Now, see if you can answer some questions about the words you just learned. Look at the picture with the number one next to it.

Number 1. Is this a *Junge* or a *Ratte*? A *Ratte*? No, this is a *Junge*, a boy.

Number 2. Is this a *Bär*? Yes, it is a *Bär*, it is a bear.

Number 3. This is a *Mädchen*, right? No, this is a *Ratte*.

Number 4. This one's a *Bär*, right? No, this one is a *Mädchen*.

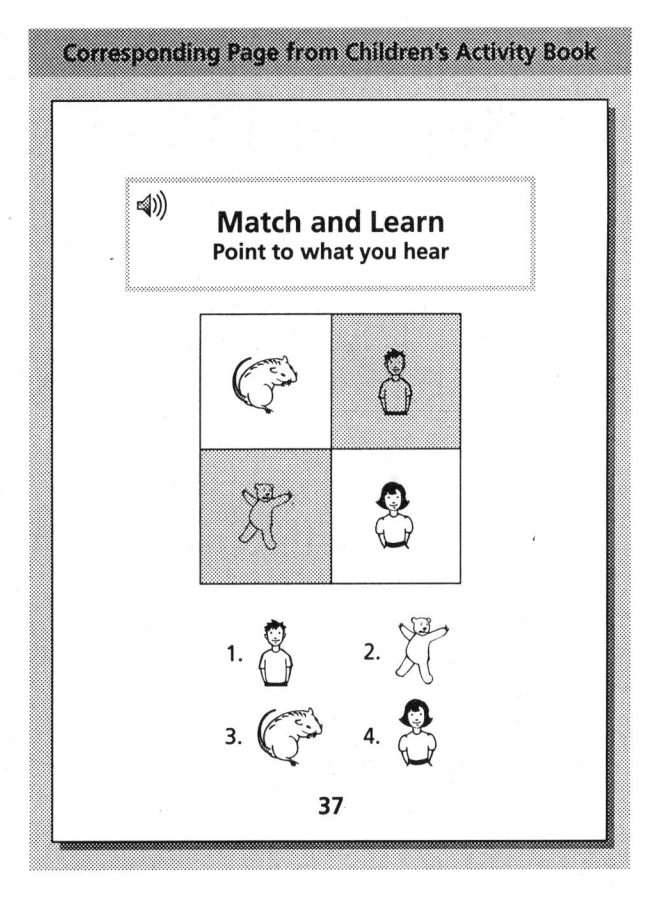

Corresponding Page from Children's Activity Book

Match and Learn
Point to what you hear

Diglot Weave

This activity begins a simple bilingual or diglot weave narrative built around two of the characters from the previous activities. This type of narrative was originally introduced as a language learning aid by Professor Rudy Lentulay of Bryn Mawr University.

Instructions for This Page

Have your children listen carefully and follow the story in their activity books as it is told on the tape.

Have your children follow the words and pictures of the story with their finger, so that when the tape says the German word for "bear," for instance, their finger is pointing to the picture of the bear. This kinesthetic connection will enhance their mental connections between the German words and the ideas they represent.

Audio Transcript

Narrator: Now listen to Wolfgang's story about a boy, a *Junge*, and a bear, a *Bär*. Follow along and look at the pictures.

Ein Junge sees *einen Bär. Der Bär* sees *den Junge. Der Bär* roars--rrr! *Der Junge* roars--rrr! *Der Bär* goes toward *dem Jungen,* roaring--rrr! *Der Junge* goes toward *dem Bär,* roaring--rrr!

Der Bär hesitates, then turns back and runs. *Der Junge* doesn't hesitate. *Der Junge* chases *den Bär.* But *der Bär* escapes.

Der Junge sits down *und lacht. Der Bär* sits down *und weint.*

Were you able to follow along? Good.

Corresponding Page from Children's Activity Book

Diglot Weave
Ein Junge und Einen Bär

- 👦 sees 🐻. 🐻 sees 👦
- 🐻 roars—rrr!
- 👦 roars—rrr!
- 🐻 goes toward 👦, roaring—rrr!
- 👦 goes toward 🐻, roaring—rrr!
- 🐻 hesitates, then turns back, and runs.
- 👦 doesn't hesitate.
- 👦 chases 🐻. But 🐻 escapes.
- 👦 🪑 and 😄.
- 🐻 🪑 and 😢.

38

Match and Learn

This activity uses frames once again to introduce some new pictures that can then be incorporated into the telling of the story.

Instructions for This Page

Have your children point to the correct pictures as the tape instructs.

Audio Transcript

Narrator: Before I tell this story again, I'll teach you some more words in German.

Look at frame 1. Point to the box with the bear and the roar sound. This is the top gray box. These two pictures together mean "bear roars." In German "bear roars" is *Bär brüllt*. Now, point to *Junge sieht Bär*, "boy sees bear." *Junge sieht Bär* is in the top white box, right? Now point to *Bär sieht Jungen*, "bear sees boy." Did you point to the bottom gray box? Good. Let's keep going.

Look at frame 2. Point to "boy goes toward." This is in the top white box. Do you see it? The big arrow next to the boy means "goes." In German it's *geht*, goes. So the picture in the top white box means *Junge geht zum*, "boy advances toward." Now point to *Bär geht zum*. It's in the top, gray box, right? Good job. Now point to *Junge jagt Bär*. It is in the bottom gray box, right? Good. Do you remember what *jagt* means? It means chases? That's right. Now point to "bear hesitates, then turns back." This picture is in the bottom white box. In German it is, *Bär zögert, dreht sich um*.

Now look at frame 3. Point to "boy sits down." The arrow pointing to the chair means "sits." In German it's *setzt*. So, point to *Junge setzt*. It's in the bottom gray box, right? Good job. Now point to *Bär setzt*. It's in the top gray box, right? Now point to "the boy does not hesitate," *Junge zögert nicht*. It's in the top white box, right?

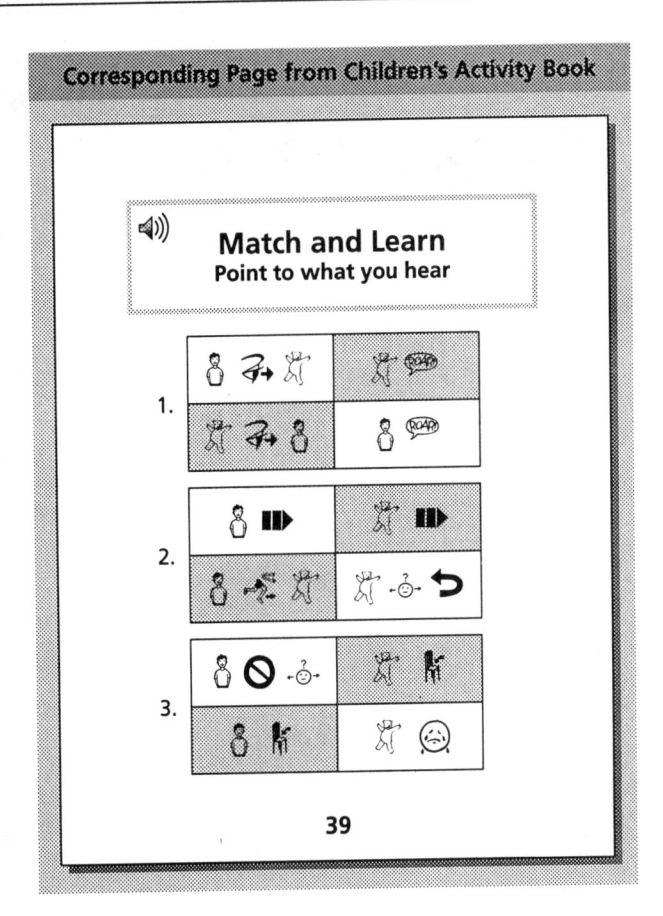

Match and Learn

This activity uses frames once again to introduce a couple more new pictures that can then be incorporated into the telling of the story.

Instructions for This Page

Have your children point to the pictures as directed by the tape.

Have your children pause the tape as needed to have time to give their answers.

Audio Transcript

Narrator: You're doing fine with these new German words. Let's learn some more.

Look at frame 4. Do you remember what "hesitates" is in German? That's right, it's *zögert*. Point to *Bär zögert*. It's in the bottom gray box, right? Now point to *Junge geht zum Bär*. It's is in the top white box, right? Good. Now point to *Junge zögert nicht*. Did you point to the top white box? Good. Now point to *Bär setzt*. It's in the bottom white box, right?

Now look at frame 5. Point to *Bär weint*. Did you point to the top gray box? That's right. Now point to *Bär zögert, dreht sich um, läuft*. Can you guess which one that is? Did you choose the top white box? Right again! Now point to *Junge setzt*. It's is in the bottom gray box, right? Good. Now point to *Junge lacht*. Did you point to the bottom white box? Good.

Now look at frame 6. Point to *Junge zögert nicht*. Did you point to the bottom white box? Good. Now point to *Bär entkommt*. "Bear escapes" is in the bottom gray box. right? Now point to *Bär setzt sich und weint*. It is in the top white box, right? Now point to *Junge jagt den Bär*. Did you point to the top gray box? Very well done!

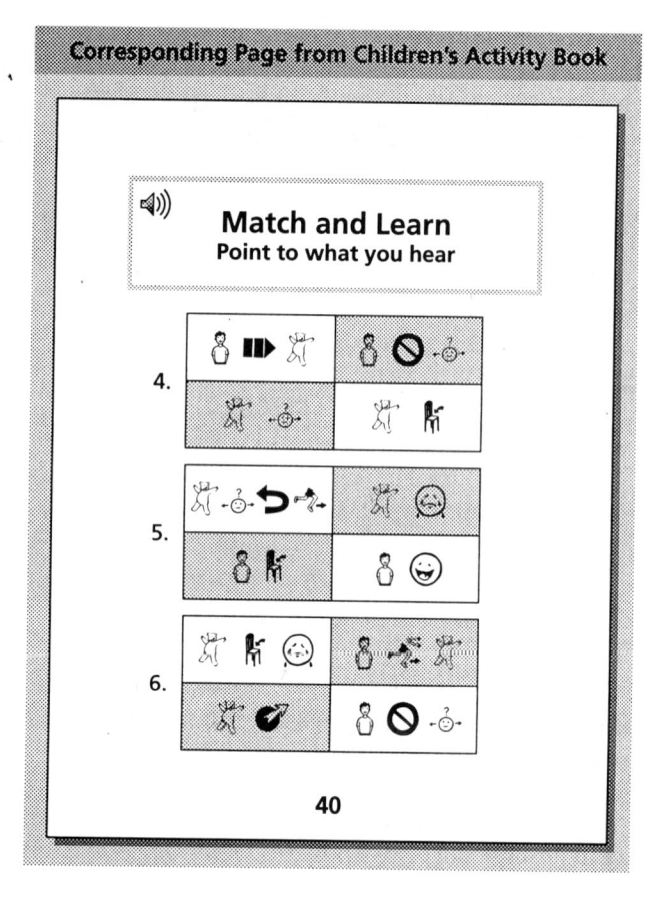

Rebus Story

This activity is designed to help your children begin to think in German. This is accomplished by having pictures in the activity book represent the German words read on the tape. This way the children will associate the German words with their English equivalents. The German words and ideas will be directly associated in their minds.

Instructions for This Page

Have your children follow the pictures with their finger as the German words for those pictures are read on the tape.

💡 This rebus story is missing two sentences near the end. See is your children can remember what happens in the story just before the boy sits down to laugh. The missing line is "The boy chases the bear. But the bear escapes."

This is a good activity for drawing pictures and creating flashcards. Encourage your children to create stories of their own!

Audio Transcript

🔊 Narrator: Now that you know the story, try to follow the pictures as I tell you the story all in German. Are you ready? Here we go!

Eine Junge sieht einen Bär. Der Bär sieht den Jungen. Der Bär brüllt--rrr! Der Junge brüllt--rrr! Der Bär geht zum Jungen, brüllt--rrr! Der Junge geht zum Bär, brüllt--rrr! Der Bär zögert, dreht sich um, läuft. Der Junge setzt sich und lacht. Der Bär setzt sich und weint.

Were you able to understand the entire story? Very good.

Corresponding Page from Children's Activity Book

Rebus Story
Eine Junge und Einen Bär

A Boy and a Bear

Describe What You See

This activity requires your children to use the German words they learned in the previous activity to describe the pictures they see.

Instructions for This Page

Have your children say the German words for the pictures, or write them on the blank lines to the side of the pictures.

> Have your children say or write in as many of the German words as they can on their own. Then you may go back through with them and help them remember those they missed. Continue to encourage them to guess when they need to, and to not feel bad when they cannot remember all the words or when they get one wrong.

Audio Transcript

Narrator: On this page are some of the pictures you have learned the words for. Say the German words for the pictures. Or if you like, write the German words for the pictures in the blanks.

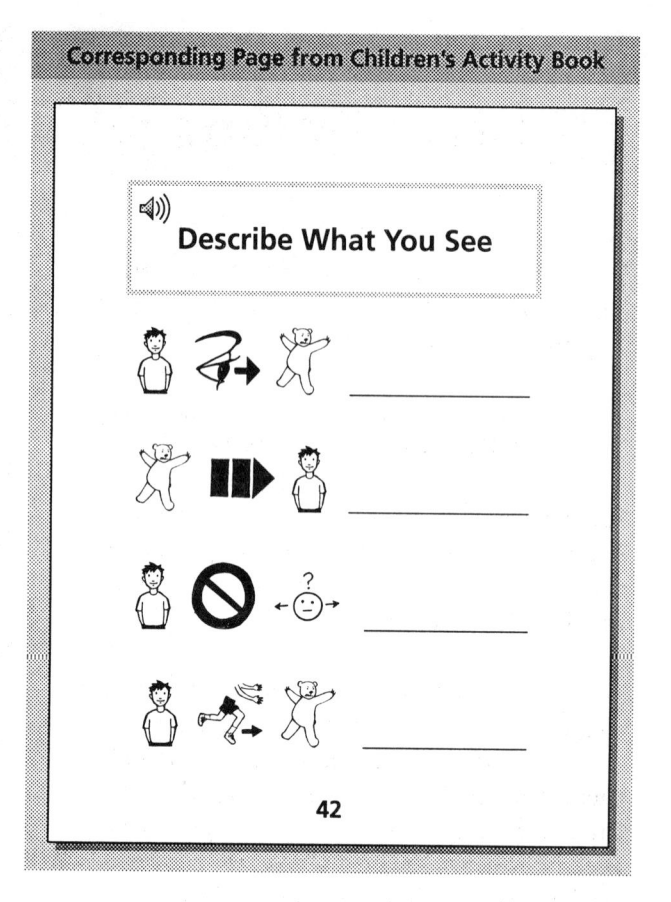

Story Telling

This activity lets your children use the German words they have learned to tell the story of "A Boy and a Bear" themselves.

Instructions for This Page

Have your children follow the trail of pictures (from top to bottom) with their finger, telling the story using the German words for the pictured items as they go.

If your children cannot remember a particular word let them think for a moment, and then go ahead and help them. Your goal here is to encourage them to think as hard as they can on their own, while keeping them from getting frustrated or discouraged. Encourage them to create their own stories using the pictures in this activity.

Audio Transcript

Narrator: Follow the trail of pictures from top to bottom with your finger, telling the story using the German words for the pictures.

Corresponding Page from Children's Activity Book

Story Telling
Look at the pictures and tell the story

Practice in German

This activity asks your children to tell the story on their own, using the German words they have learned, and using the pictures in the circle as memory prompts.

Instructions for This Page

Have your children look at the pictures in the circle and try to tell the story on their own, using the German words they have leaned. Have them record how long it takes them to tell the complete story in German their first time, and then their best subsequent time.

💡 Let your children try telling the story as many as six or eight times, each time trying to improve their speed.

Audio Transcript

🔊 Narrator: Last of all, use the pictures in the big circle on your activity book page to tell the story again, using the German words you have learned. Point to the pictures as you go along, and write down in the first box how long it takes you to tell the story the first time. Then tell the story a few more times, and write down your fastest time in the second box.

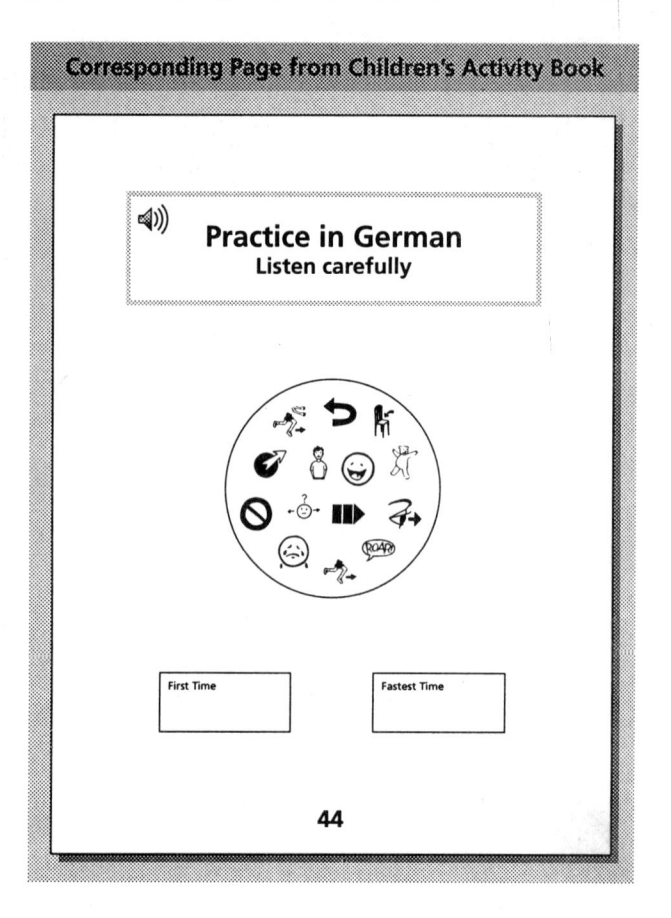

Making Gingerbread Men

This section contains an audio transcript of the adventure story your children will hear on the tape.

Instructions for This Page

Have your children listen carefully as the adventure story is read on the tape. Encourage your children to take an active part in listening to the adventure story. Ask them to respond to things they hear and have them say out loud words said by the characters on the tape.

Younger children might enjoy coloring the picture as the adventure story is read. Older children may want to follow along with the written audio transcript provided in this *Parent's Guide*.

Audio Transcript

Narrator 2: The Adventure Continues: Making Gingerbread Men

Narrator: "That's a good story, Wolfgang," you say when he is finished. "Thanks for telling it to us."

Max: Yeah. The boy in that story was really brave. He didn't even get worried when he was facing a roaring bear!

Wolfgang: That's right, Max. And that's the next piece of your treasure: DON'T STRESS. Don't worry about how fast you're learning, or even if you are remembering everything you've learned. If you put too much pressure on yourself, learning becomes a burden, and you actually remember less and don't let yourself guess what things mean. It's works much better to just let the language come to you.

Serena: Don't stress. OK. That makes three now: Build on what you know, Make learning fun, and Don't stress.

Wolfgang: Excellent memory. And now, don't you think it's about time to head for home? I imagine dinner time is almost here. I'm ready to close the zoo and go home myself! It's been a pleasure showing you around. Thank you for all your help with the animals!

Max: Thank you, Wolfgang, for letting us help!

Narrator: "Yeah," you agree. "And thank you for telling us that story!"

Wolfgang: You're all very welcome. I hope to see you again. Good luck on the rest of your adventures here in the valley!

Serena: *Danke schön,* Wolfgang!

Max: *Ja. Danke schön!*

Narrator: You, Serena and Max get back to Nicole and Dieter's house just in time for dinner, and as you're eating Nicole says:

Continued from Children's Activity Book, page 45

Nicole: Well, have you had any good adventures today?

Narrator: "Yes," you reply, "we sure have."

Max: Yeah. The map you gave us led us to the zoo, and we met a really friendly zoo keeper who took us around and showed us all the animals and stuff.

Serena: Yeah, and he told us a story, too, and all about Luxembourg!

Dieter: That must be Wolfgang, *ja?*

Max: Yeah. That was his name. Do you know him?

Dieter: Of course. He is a good friend of mine. Did he teach you how to say the names of the different parts of the animal's bodies in German?

Serena: You mean like the names for their heads and arms and legs and stuff?

Dieter: That's right.

Serena: No, his didn't tell us that. Could you teach us those words?

Dieter: Yes. And if I'm right, Nicole might have a way to make learning them really enjoyable. What do you think, Nicole, should we share our gingerbread cookies recipe with them?

Nicole: Oh, yes. That's a perfect idea, Dieter. Let's all make gingerbread men, and while we eat them, I can teach you the words for body parts, all right?

Max: That sounds great to me! I love cookies!

Narrator: "Me too," you agree.

Serena: And me.

Narrator: So, after quickly cleaning up from dinner, you, Serena, Max, Nicole and Dieter all begin making gingerbread cookies. You mix the ingredients, roll out the dough, cut the cookies into the shapes of people, and bake them until they are just right. "Mmmm! These are *lecker,"* you say, remembering the word Heidi had used the day before.

Nicole: *Danke schön.* And now, let me teach you the German words for body parts.

Body Parts

This activity is designed to teach your children the German words for parts of the body. It incorporates kinesthetic associations, drawing and matching activities in going over the body part words several times.

This first activity introduces the basic body parts.

Instructions for This Page

Have your children look at the picture of the gingerbread man cookie in their activity book and point to the parts of the cookie's body as the tape directs them.

Encourage your children to say the German words out loud as they point to each body part.

Learning singular and plural forms of German words is sometimes difficult. We use both forms interchangeably to allow your children to identify the body part. They will learn the various forms of words later on in their language study.

Audio Transcript

Narrator 2: Activity: Body Parts.

Narrator: Here are the words for body parts that Nicole teaches you. As I say the German word for each part, point to that part and repeat the German word. Ready? OK. Here we go!

Point to the cookie's head. The German word for "head" is *Kopf*. Say it out loud while pointing at the head: *Kopf, Kopf*.

Now point to the cookie's body. The "body" is called the *Körper*. Say it out loud: *Körper, Körper*.

Corresponding Page from Children's Activity Book

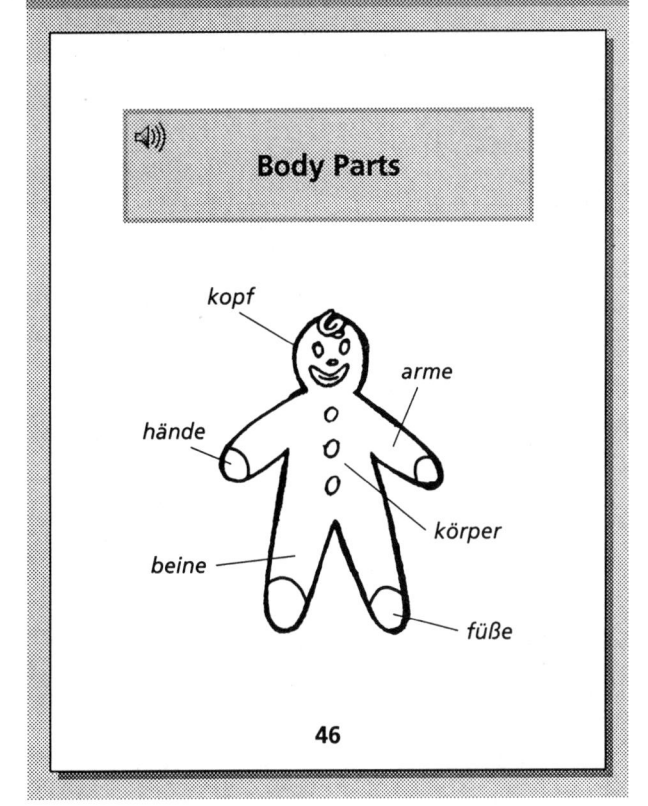

Body Parts

- kopf
- arme
- hände
- körper
- beine
- füße

46

Now point to the arms. "Arms" in German are called *Arme*. Say those out loud: *Arme, Arme*.

Now point to the cookie's hands: its *Hände*. Say *Hände* out loud: *Hände, Hände*.

Now, point to the cookie's legs. The German word for legs is *Beine*. Say it out loud: *Beine, Beine*.

Finally, point to the cookie's feet. In German feet are called *Füße*. Say it out loud: *Füße, Füße*.

Did you point to each part and say the German word for it out loud? Good! Now you know the words for the basic parts of the body. As we go along, you'll learn them even better!

Match and Learn

This activity reviews the basic body parts your children have just been introduced to by showing cookies with some parts missing (eaten) and asking them to point to the cookies with the specified missing parts.

Instructions for This Page

Have your children look at the pictures of partly eaten cookies and point to the ones with those missing parts indicated on the tape.

💡 A fun extension of this activity would be to make cookies shaped like people and have your children say the name of each body part as they eat it—a good review and a yummy treat!

Audio Transcript

🔊 Narrator: To help you review the German words you have just learned, try looking at the partly eaten cookies on your activity book page and pointing to the ones I describe.

Point to the cookie without a *Kopf*. Did you point to the cookie without a head? Good.

Now point to the cookie that is missing one *Arm*. Did you point to the cookie with only one arm? Good.

Now point to the cookie with no *Hände* at all. Did you point to the one without any hands? Good.

Now find the cookie that has only one *Bein*. Did you find the one with only one leg? Good.

OK, now point to the cookie with a head, arms and legs, but no *Körper*. Did you pick the one without a body? Good.

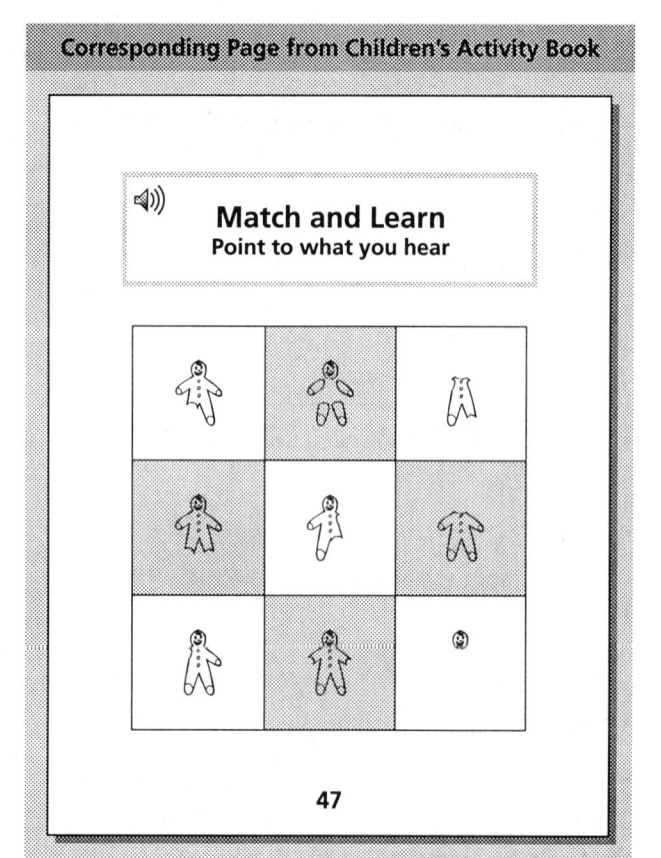

Corresponding Page from Children's Activity Book

🔊 **Match and Learn**
Point to what you hear

47

Now point to the cookie with missing *Füße*. Did you point to the cookie that doesn't have any feet? Good.

Now find a cookie with only one *Arm*, and only one *Bein*. Did you find the cookie with only one arm and only one leg? Good.

Now see if you can find a cookie with only one *Fuße*, no *Kopf*, and no *Arme*. Did you find the one with only one foot, no head, and no arms? Good.

Finally, can you see a cookie with a *Kopf*, but no *Körper* to go with it? Did you pick the one that is just a head? That's the right one!

Draw and Learn

This activity invites your children to draw a cookie of their own based on instructions given using German body part words.

Instructions for This Page

Have your children draw simple figures of their own, part by part as the tape directs. Have your children pause the tape as needed to have time for drawing.

💡 Encourage your children to draw whatever kind of person they are comfortable with and interested in. For example, they can draw a cookie or a stick figure, a boy or a girl, a very simple figure or a more detailed, colorful one. Since the activity is designed simply to reinforce their memory of the German words, let them do whatever makes it fun for them.

Audio Transcript

🔊 Narrator: Now that you know the German words for parts of the body, it's your turn to draw! Use a crayon, pencil, pen or marker to draw the parts of a person on the chalkboard as I say them in German. You can stop the tape and go get something to draw with if you need to. Are you ready to draw? All right, here we go!

First, draw a *Kopf*. Are you finished? Good!

Now, add to the *Kopf* a *Körper*. OK.

Now add *Beine* to the *Körper*.

And add *Füße* where they go.

Now add *Arme* where they go.

Corresponding Page from Children's Activity Book

🔊 **Draw and Learn**
Draw what you hear

48

Have you done all that? Good! What's left? *Hände?* Right!

Add *Hände* where they go. Are you done? All right. That should do it!

Now that your person is all drawn, fill it in or color it however you want. When you're done, turn the page to see an example of what you might have drawn.

Draw and Learn

This page contains a sample drawing for your children to compare theirs to, and it also reinforces the German body part words.

Instructions for This Page

Have your children look at the picture of the gingerbread man cookie in their activity book and compare it to their drawing on the previous page. Have them look at the body parts as they are reviewed on the tape a final time.

If your children need more practice with the basic body parts, rewind the tape and let them try drawing figures a few more times.

Audio Transcript

Narrator: Here is a cookie that looks kind of like the one you just drew. It has all the body parts: a head—a *Kopf*, a body—a *Körper*, legs—*Beine*, arms—*Arme*, hands—*Hände*, and feet—*Füße*. You can color this cookie now, if you like.

Match and Learn

This activity tests your children's memory of the German body part words learned so far.

Instructions for This Page

Have your children look at the Match and Learn frames and point to the appropriate pictures as the German words are read on the tape. Have your children pause the tape as needed to have time to give their answers.

Encourage your children to guess boldly in this activity. If they guess wrong, they will usually have a chance to try again in a subsequent frame.

Audio Transcript

Narrator: You've learned those German words very quickly. Do you think you can remember them all? Let's see! In each frame, point to what you hear.

Look at frame 1. Point to the *Hände*. Did you point to the hand? Good! Now point to the *Kopf*. Did you point to the head? Good! Finally, point to the *Bein*. Did you point to the leg? That's right.

Now look at frame 2. First, point to the *Arm*. Did you point to the arm? That's right! Now point to the *Körper*. Did you point to the body? Well done. Finally, point to the *Fuß*. Did you point to the foot? Good.

Now look at frame 3. Can you see a *Bein*? Did you choose the leg? That's right. Now, can you see a *Kopf*? Did you point to the head? Correct! And last, do you see a *Hand* here? Yes? It's a hand right?

Now look at frame 4. Point to the *Körper*. Are you pointing to the body? Now point to the *Arm*. Did you point to the arm? Now point to the *Fuß*. Did you choose the foot? Good.

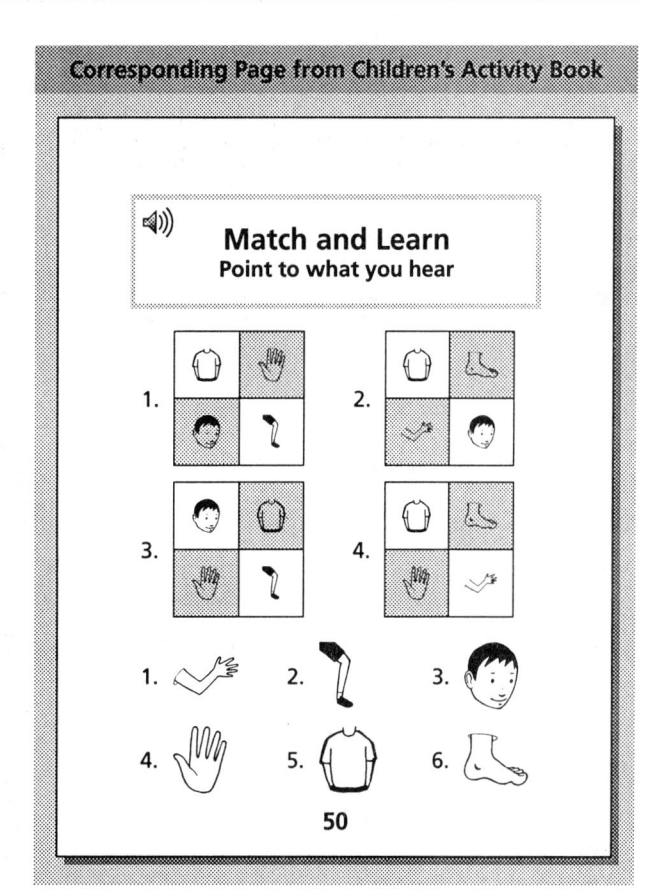

Now look at the numbered pictures at the bottom of the page. As I say the English word for each picture, say the German word for that picture out loud.

Number 1. Arm. Did you say *Arm*? Good.

Number 2. Leg. Did you say *Bein*? Good.

Number 3. Head. Did you say *Kopf*? Good.

Number 4. Hand. Did you say *Hand*? Good.

Number 5. Body. Did you say *Körper*? Good.

Number 6. Foot. Did you say *Fuß*? Well done.

Draw and Learn

This activity teaches your children the German word for fingers in a fun way by letting them trace around their own fingers.

Instructions for This Page

Have your children trace their hand in the chalkboard space on their activity book pages.

Audio Transcript

Narrator: Now that you know all those words, it is time for a new one: the German word for fingers. "Fingers" in German are called *Finger*. To help you learn this word, I'd like you to trace your hand on the chalkboard on your page. This is easy to do, and you have probably even done it before. All you need to do is put your hand down on the page right in the middle of the chalkboard, and trace around it with a crayon or a pencil. Go ahead and trace your hand now.

Corresponding Page from Children's Activity Book

Draw and Learn
Trace your hand

51

Draw and Learn

This page contains a sample of what your children's hand tracing may have looked like. This page also reinforces both the German word for fingers and the German numbers one through five by having your children count the fingers on the sample hand.

Instructions for This Page

Have your children compare their tracing to the sample on this page. Then have them point to the fingers one by one and count out loud as they are counted on the tape.

> If your children would like, they may turn back to the previous page and count the fingers of their own drawing.

Audio Transcript

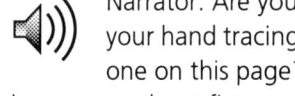

Narrator: Are you finished? Good. Does your hand tracing look something like the one on this page? Wonderful! Now let's learn more about fingers.

How many fingers—how many *Finger*—does your hand have? Five? That's right! Let's count the *Finger* in German. *Ein Finger, zwei Finger, drei Finger, vier Finger, fünf Finger!* Let's count them one more time. *Ein Finger, zwei Finger, drei Finger, vier Finger, fünf Finger!*

Corresponding Page from Children's Activity Book

52

Face Parts

This next part of the activity is designed to teach your children the German words for parts of the face. The following activities incorporate kinesthetic associations, drawing, matching and singing in going over the new words several times.

Instructions for This Page

Have your children look at the picture of the boy's face in their activity book and point to the parts of the face as the tape directs them.

💡 Encourage your children to say the German words out loud as they point to each part.

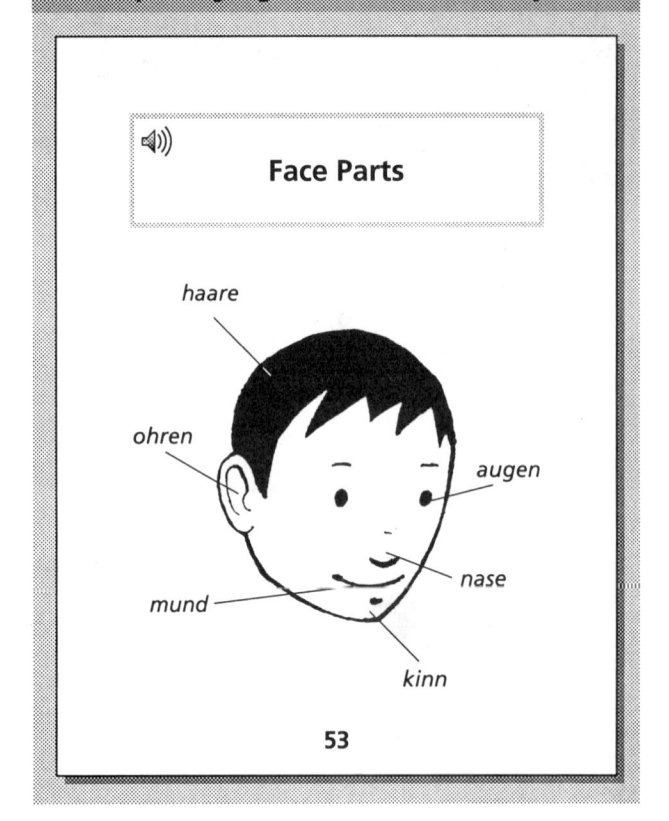

Audio Transcript

🔊 Narrator: Now that you know the German words for parts of your body, you're ready to learn the words for parts of your face. Look at the face of the boy on your activity book page and point to the different parts as I tell you their names in English and German.

Point to the boy's eyes. The German word for "eyes" is *Augen*. Say it out loud: *Augen, Augen*.

Now point to the boy's nose. The word for "nose" in German is *Nase*. Say it out loud: *Nase, Nase*.

Now point to the boy's ears. The German word for "ears" is *Ohren*. Say it out loud: *Ohren, Ohren*.

Now point to the boy's mouth—his *Mund*. *Mund* is the German word for mouth. Say it out loud: *Mund, Mund*.

Now point to the boy's hair. The German word for hair is *Haare*. *Haare* means hair. Say it out loud: *Haare, Haare*.

Now point to the boy's chin. The German word for "chin" is *Kinn*. Say it out loud: *Kinn, Kinn*.

Can you remember all those? I'll go through them quickly one more time. Point to what you hear. First, the *Augen*—eyes. Next, the *Nase*—the nose. Now the *Ohren*—ears, and the *Mund*—the mouth. Now point to the *Haare*—hair; and finally, the *Kinn*, the chin. Did you point to each one? Very good!

Corresponding Page from Children's Activity Book

Face Parts

- haare
- ohren
- augen
- mund
- nase
- kinn

53

Draw and Learn

This activity is designed to reinforce the German words for parts of the face in a fun way by having your children draw them.

Instructions for This Page

Have your children draw parts of the face on the oval shown in their work book as the tape directs them. Have your children pause the tape as needed to have time for drawing.

Encourage your children to be creative and draw whatever type of face they want, provided the parts are those called for on the tape.

Audio Transcript

Narrator: Now that you've learned those words, let's try drawing a face. On your activity book page there is a blank face ready to color on. As I say the words in German, draw the things I say on the blank face. Are you ready to draw? OK!

First draw a *Mund* on the face. Are you finished? Good. Did you draw a mouth? That's right!

Now draw *Augen* on the face. Are you finished? Did you draw two eyes? Good!

Now draw *Ohren* where they go. Did you draw ears on the sides? Good.

Now drawn a *Nase* on the face. Does your face have a nose now? Good.

Now draw *Haare* where it goes. Did you draw hair? That's right!

And that's all, except, of course, for the *Kinn*—but the face already has a kind of *Kinn*! (You can draw a better one if you want to.)

Corresponding Page from Children's Activity Book

Draw and Learn
Draw what you hear

Match and Learn

This activity tests your children's memory of the German face part words they have learned.

Instructions for This Page

Have your children look at the match and learn frames and point to the appropriate pictures as the German words are read on the tape.

Encourage your children to guess boldly in this activity. If they guess wrong, they will usually have a chance to try again in a subsequent frame.

Audio Transcript

Narrator: You've learned those German words very quickly. Do you think you can remember them all? Let's see! In each frame, point to what you hear.

Look at frame 1. Point to *das Kinn*. Did you point to the chin? Good! Now point to *das Auge*. Did you point to the eye? Good. Finally, point to *das Ohr*. Did you point to the ear? Well done.

Now look at frame 2. First, point to *den Mund*. Did you point to the mouth? Now point to *die Nase*. Did you point to the nose? Good. Finally, point to *die Haare*. Did you point to the hair? Good.

Now look at frame 3. Point to *ein Ohr*? Did you point to an ear? Now, point to *ein Auge*. Did you point to the eye? Good. And last, do you see *ein Kinn* here? Is it a chin? That's right.

Now look at frame 4. Point to *die Hand* with *drei Finger* up. Are you pointing to the hand with three fingers up? Now point to *die Hand* with *fünf Finger* up. Did you point to the hand with all five fingers up? Very good. Now point to *die Hand* with

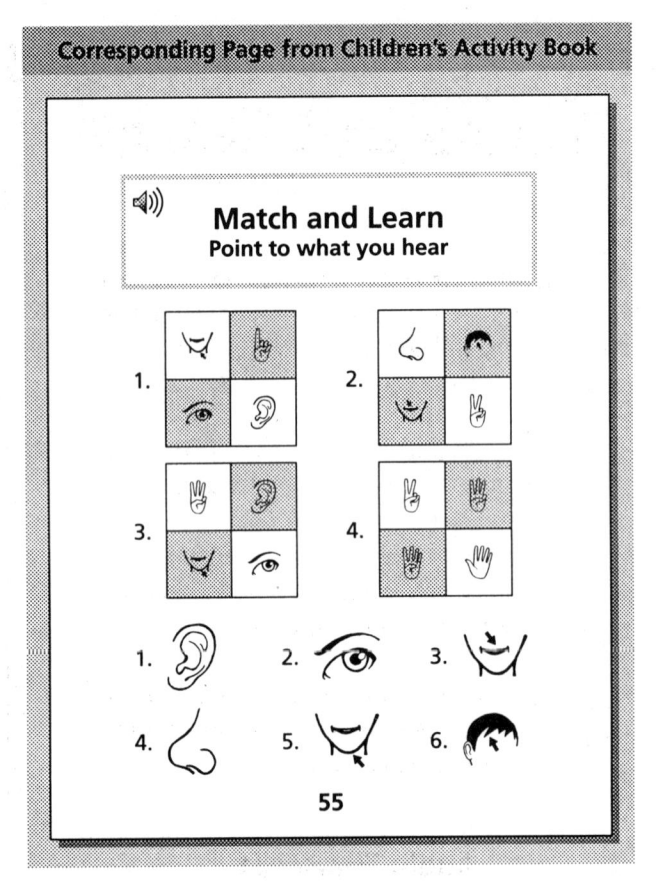

Corresponding Page from Children's Activity Book

Match and Learn
Point to what you hear

vier Finger up. Did you choose the one with four fingers up? That's right!

Now look at the numbered pictures at the bottom of the page. As I say the English word for each picture, say the German word for that picture out loud.

Number 1. Ear. Did you say *Ohr?* Good.

Number 2. Eye. Did you say *Auge?* Good.

Number 3. Mouth. Did you say *Mund?* Good.

Number 4. Nose. Did you say *Nase?* Good.

Number 5. Chin. Did you say *Kinn?* Good.

Number 6. Hair. Did you say *Haare?* That's exactly right.

Body Parts   P–72   Match and Learn

Touch and Learn

This activity tests and reinforces your children's memory of the German body part and face part words they have learned by having them touch those parts of their own bodies and faces.

Instructions for This Page

Have your children listen to the German words said on the tape and touch the parts of their bodies and faces that the tape directs.

Encourage your children to stand up and have fun with this activity. Encourage them to guess boldly.

Audio Transcript

Narrator: You've now learned the German words for all the main parts of your body and your face. Do you think you can remember them all? Let's see! Stand up, and as I say the German word for a part of your body or your face, touch it. For example, if I say: "Touch your *Kopf*," you should touch your head.

Let's try a few.

Touch your *Nase*. Did you touch your nose? Good.

Now touch your *Arme*. Did you touch your arms? That's right.

Now touch your *Füße*. Did you touch your feet? Good.

Now touch your *Körper*. Did you touch your body? Good job.

Now touch your *Mund*. Did you touch your mouth? Right.

Now touch your *Kinn*. Did you touch your chin! Good.

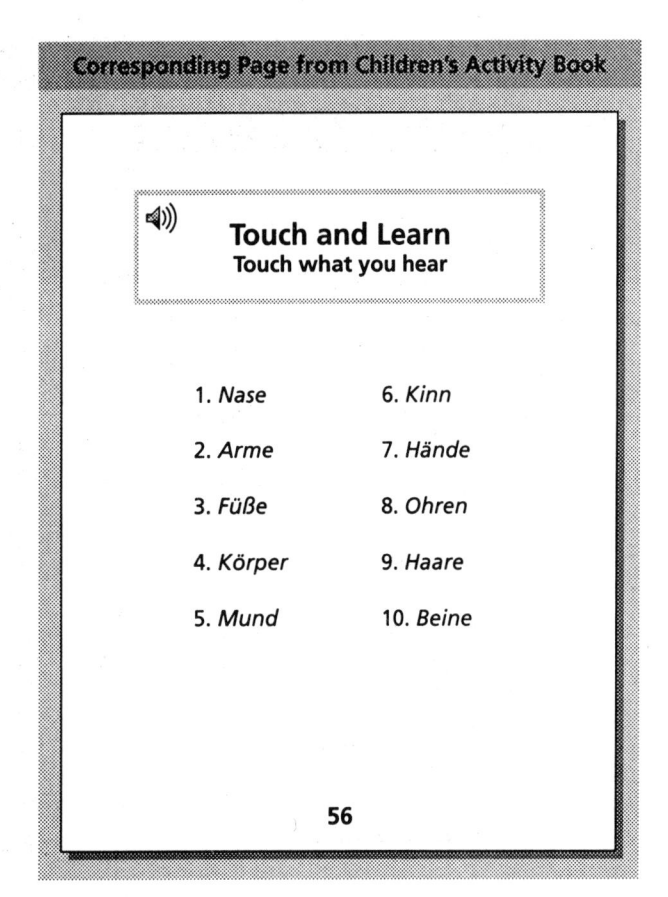

Corresponding Page from Children's Activity Book

Touch and Learn
Touch what you hear

1. *Nase*   6. *Kinn*
2. *Arme*   7. *Hände*
3. *Füße*   8. *Ohren*
4. *Körper*   9. *Haare*
5. *Mund*   10. *Beine*

56

Now touch your *Hände*. Did you touch your *Hände* with your *Hand*? I'll bet you did! Your *Hände* are your hands, right?

Now touch your *Ohren*. Did you touch your ears? Good.

Now touch your *Haare*. Did you touch your hair? Right on.

Now touch your *Beine*. Did you touch your legs? Excellent!

Sing and Learn

In this activity your children use the words they have learned to sing an action song. This reinforces the words in their memory one last time, and makes learning them fun.

Instructions for This Page

Have your children listen to the song on the tape once completely through, then on the second, third and fourth times, have them try to sing along and touch the body parts sung in the song.

💡 Many children enjoy action songs very much, and they are one of the best ways to reinforce words in memory. Encourage your children to make up their own body parts songs!

Audio Transcript

Narrator: Now that you've learned the German words for all those parts of your body, you're ready to sing a song using them. The first time through, just listen to the song and think of the body parts that the words stand for. Then the second time through stand up and try to sing along and touch the parts of your body as you say them. Start out singing the song slowly, and then speed up until, on the third or fourth time, you're singing it as fast as you can!

The song goes like this. Remember, just listen this first time.

Kopf, Körper, Beine, Füße,
   Beine, Füße, Beine, Füße,
Kopf, Körper, Beine, Füße,
   Augen, Ohren, Nase und Mund.

Were you able to follow along? Good!

Now stand up and try to sing along and touch the right parts of your body as you sing the words for them in the song! This time we will sing the song together slowly.

Kopf, Körper, Beine, Füße,
   Beine, Füße, Beine, Füße,
Kopf, Körper, Beine, Füße,
   Augen, Ohren, Nase und Mund.

How did you do? Were you able to keep up? Now again, a little faster:

Kopf, Körper, Beine, Füße,
   Beine, Füße, Beine, Füße,
Kopf, Körper, Beine, Füße,
   Augen, Ohren, Nase und Mund.

Did you keep up that time too? Wow, you're quick! All right, one more time, really fast.

Kopf, Körper, Beine, Füße,
   Beine, Füße, Beine, Füße,
Kopf, Körper, Beine, Füße,
   Augen, Ohren, Nase und Mund.

Wow! That was fast. I'm tired—how about you? Well, now you know an easy way to remember some of the German words you've just learned.

Corresponding Page from Children's Activity Book

🔊 **Sing and Learn**
Do the actions as you sing

Kopf, Körper, Beine, Füße,
Beine, Füße, Beine, Füße,
Kopf, Körper, Beine, Füße,
Augen, Ohren, Nase und Mund.

57

Harvesting Yams on a Farm

This section contains an audio transcript of the adventure story your children will hear on the tape.

Instructions for This Page

Have your children listen carefully as the adventure story is read on the tape. Encourage your children to take an active part in listening to the adventure story. Ask them to respond to things they hear and have them say out loud words said by the characters on the tape.

Younger children might enjoy coloring the picture as the adventure story is read. Older children may want to follow along with the written audio transcript provided in this *Parent's Guide*.

Audio Transcript

Narrator 2: The Adventure Continues: Harvesting Yams on a Farm

Serena: Thanks for teaching us all those new words, Nicole.

Narrator: "Yeah," you say, holding back a yawn. "It's fun to learn the way you teach. But boy, I'm really tired."

Max: <yawning> Me too.

Dieter: Yes. I think it's time for all of us to say *Guten Nacht.* I'll see you in the morning, my friends, unless I'm mistaken. *Guten Nacht!*

Max: *Guten Nacht,* Dieter!

Serena: *Ja. Guten Nacht!*

Narrator: Back up in the loft you, Serena and Max are all asleep within minutes. The next morning, however, you are puzzled to find that Dieter has already gone. You ask Nicole about him.

Nicole: Yes, he was up quite early this morning, and he left nearly three hours ago.

Max: But didn't he say we'd see him this morning? I don't get it. Well, we'll just have to look for the next spot on our map I guess!

Narrator: "Yeah," you say. "I'm excited to go across the valley to the table. See, here on the map the next spot we have to go to is on the other side of the open farmlands beyond the village. The spot looks like it's on an island right in the middle of the big lake!"

Max: Yeah, you're right. That will be cool to go farther than we ever have. The farms go right to the edge of the big lake, and from there we'll have to find a boat, I guess!

Nicole: Yes. There is a ferry that goes to and from that island each day. And who knows, perhaps you will still see Dieter this morning after all!

Continued from Children's Activity Book, page 59

Narrator: After breakfast you, Max and Serena set out. You walk first to the village, past the market and the zoo, and then out into the farmlands beyond.

Max: Look at these big farms. The trees have all been cleared away and it's just rolling hills. It's really green and beautiful!

Serena: Yeah. The forest is cool, but this is really nice. It feels so open and free. And look, if you kind of squint you can even see the lake in the distance!

Narrator: The three of you stare for a few minutes at the lush green farmland stretching out in front of you. You can just see the lake beyond. After a bit Serena takes out your map.

Serena: It looks like the place we need to get to is still a bit over that way. Let's go!

Narrator: The three of you keep moving along the road that winds through the farms. As you come up over the top of a small rise, you see several people harvesting yams in a field just ahead. One of them looks up as you approach, and waves.

Dieter: *Guten Tag*, my friends! *Wie geht's euch?*

Max: *Guten Tag*, Dieter! We're doing great!

Serena: We didn't expect to find you here though!

Dieter: Didn't I say I'd probably see you this morning? I knew that on your way to the next spot on your map you would have to pass this way. Come and help us harvest!

Narrator: "Are all these people here to help you harvest yams?" you ask.

Dieter: Yes. The harvest is a very important time. Our farmer friends need all the help they can get. Come and join in, and while we work I'll tell you a story about a farmer, a giant turnip, and a mouse.

Narrator: You, Serena and Max have never helped with a harvest before, and with all the people digging the yams together, it looks really exciting. Soon you are digging beside Dieter, pulling huge yams out of the rich soil. As you dig, Dieter begins telling you his story.

The Farmer and the Turnip

It is important for children to first understand spoken language, but it is more exciting when they begin to use it, and that is where the learning really takes off. In this activity we continue with comprehension building, but as the activities progress, we gradually introduce conversation.

Your children will hear a story about a farmer and a turnip several times. They will learn the character names and identify them with pictures. By the time we get to their telling the story, they will have learned to recognize the pictures well enough that they can pretty much tell the story simply by looking at the pictures.

This story is more challenging than the previous story, "A Boy and a Bear," and the discussion of the story on the tape uses more German.

Instructions for This Page

Have your children look at the first page of the story "The Farmer and the Turnip" and listen to the introduction to the story on the tape.

Audio Transcript

Narrator 2: Activity: The Farmer and the Turnip.

Narrator: The story Dieter tells you is called "The Farmer and the Turnip."

Power-Glide **Children's German**

Match and Learn

This activity is visual, audio, and kinesthetic. It is designed to help your children learn by listening and pointing.

Instructions for This Page

Have your children point to the correct boxes and pictures as the tape instructs. In the second part of the activity have them answer out loud the questions asked about the numbered pictures.

Have your children pause the tape as needed to have time to give their answers.

Audio Transcript

Narrator: Before I tell you *diese Geschichte*, I'll teach you some new words to help you understand. Look at the frame with the white and gray boxes.

Look at frame 1. Point to the seed, *der Samen*. *Der Samen* is in the top white box, right? Now point to the farmer, *der Bauer*. *Der Bauer* is in the bottom gray box, right? Point to the turnip, *die Rübe*. Is *die Rübe* in the top gray box? No, *die Rübe*, the turnip, is in the bottom white box, right? Yes. Now point to the plant, *die Pflanze*. It is in the top gray box, right?

Now look at frame 2. Point to *die Pflanze*. It is in the bottom white box, right? Now point to *der Bauer*. He is in the top white box, right? Point to the seed, *der Samen*. It is in the bottom gray box, right? Now point to *der Hund*, the dog. It is in the top gray box.

Now look at frame 3. Point to *der Hund*, the dog. It is in the top gray box, right? No, *der Hund* is in the bottom gray box. Now point to *der Samen*. It is in the top gray box, right? Yes. Point to *die Katze*, the cat. It is in the top white box, right? Yes. Now point to *der Bauer*. He is in the bottom gray box, right? No, he is in the bottom white box.

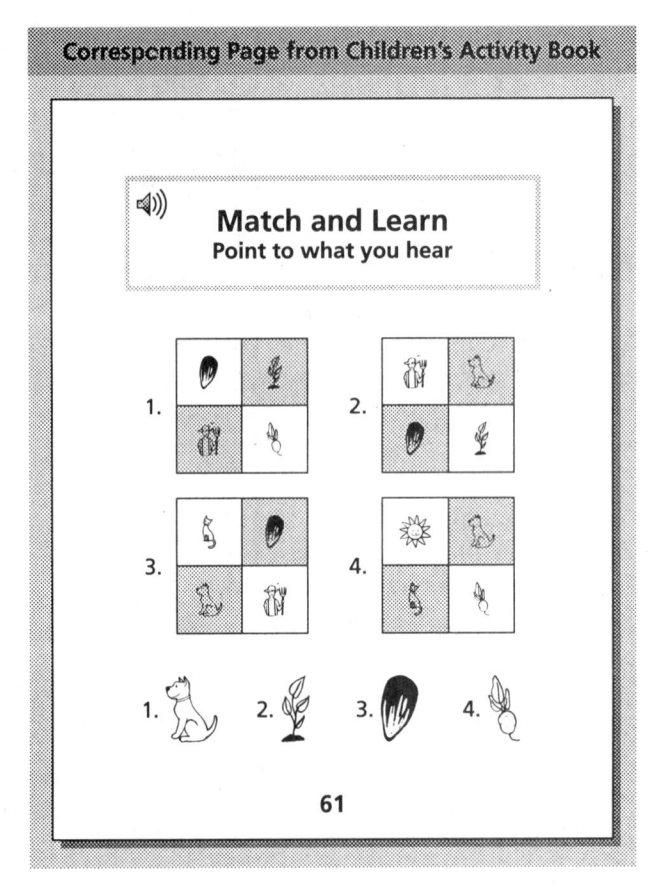

Now look at frame 4. Point to the turnip, *die Rübe*. *die Rübe* is in the bottom white box, right? Yes. Now point to *der Hund*, the dog. *Der Hund* is in the top gray box, right? Point to *die Sonne*, the sun. *Die Sonne* is in the bottom gray box, right? No, *die Sonne* is in the top white box. Now point to *die Katze*. *Die Katze* is in the bottom gray box.

Now see if you can answer some questions about the words you just learned. Look at the picture with the number one next to it.

Number 1. *Ist das ein Hund? Ja, das ist ein Hund.*

Number 2. *Ist das eine Pflanze? Ja, das ist eine Pflanze.*

Number 3. *Ist das ein Samen oder eine Rübe?* Did you say a seed, *ein Samen? Ja, das ist ein Samen.*

Number 4. *Ist das eine Pflanze? Nein, das ist eine Rübe.*

The Farmer and the Turnip

Power-Glide **Children's German**

Match and Learn

This activity uses frames once again to introduce some new pictures and German words that can then be incorporated into the telling of the story.

Instructions for This Page

Have your children point to the correct pictures as the tape instructs. In the second part of the activity have them answer out loud the questions asked about the numbered pictures.

As these activities become progressively more challenging, the main objective is to help your children feel confident. They should not be overly concerned with correctness. Encourage them to point boldly as soon as they hear what to point to in the first part of the activity, and to speak out loud in response to the questions in the second half. When your children guess wrong, let them know it's okay and to keep making their best guesses.

Audio Transcript

Narrator: Did you do well with those pictures and words? Let's try a few more.

Look at frame 5. Point to *die Pflanze*. *Die Pflanze*, the plant, is in the top gray box, right? Now point to *der Samen*. *Der Samen* is in the bottom white box, right? No, it is in the bottom gray box. Point to *die Rübe*. *Die Rübe* is in the bottom white box, right? Now point to *der Bauer* and his *Frau*, his wife. They are in the top white box, right? Yes!

Now look at frame 6. Point to *der Bauer* and *die Katze*. They are in the top gray box, right? Yes. Now point to *der Bauer* and *die Frau*. They are in the bottom gray box, right? No, they are in the top white box. Point to *der Hund* and *der Bauer*. The dog and the farmer, *der Hund und der Bauer*, are in the bottom gray box, right? Yes. Now point to *der Bauer* and *die Rübe*. They are in the bottom white box.

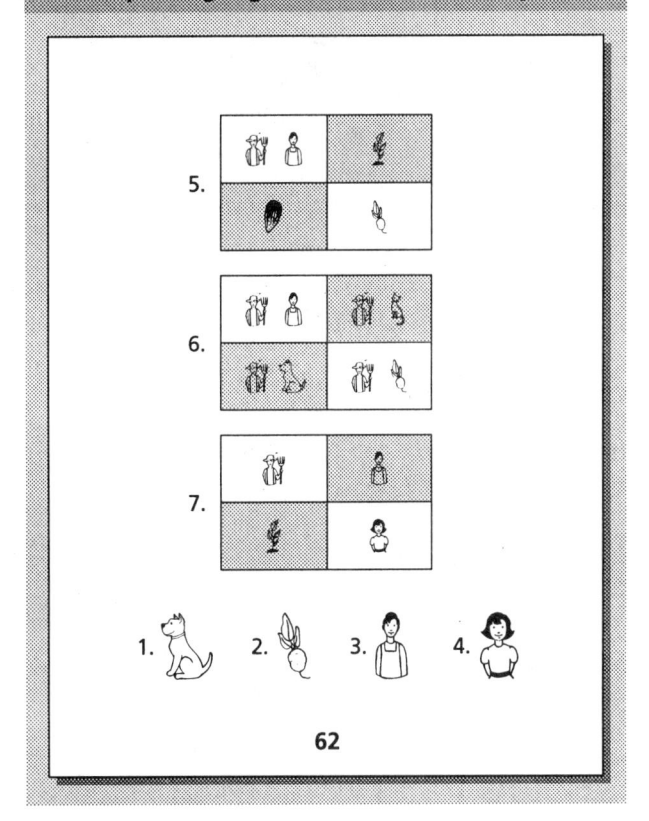

Now look at frame 7. Point to the farmer's *Tochter*, his daughter. *Die Tochter* is in the bottom white box, right? Yes, she is. Now point to *die Frau*. She is in the top gray box, right? Yes. Point to *die Pflanze*. It is in the bottom white box, right? No, it is in the bottom gray box. Now point to *der Bauer*. He is in the top white box, right? Yes.

Now, see if you can answer some questions about the words you just learned.

Look at picture number 1. *Ist es ein Hund? Ja, es ist ein Hund.*

Picture number 2. *Ist es ein Bauer oder eine Rübe? Es ist eine Rübe.*

Picture number 3. *Ist es eine Tochter? Nein, es ist eine Frau.*

Picture number 4. *Ist es eine Tochter? Ja, es ist eine Tochter.*

The Farmer and the Turnip

Diglot Weave

The following multi-page activity contains an extended diglot weave narrative built around the words from the previous activities.

Instructions for This Page

Have your children listen carefully and follow the story in their activity books as it is told on the tape.

> Have your children follow the words and pictures of the story with their finger, so that when the tape says the German word for "girl," for instance, their finger is pointing to the picture of the girl. This kinesthetic connection will enhance their mental connections between the German words and the ideas they represent.

If the pace is ever too fast, stop the tape and review with your children. Be sure to reward understanding and encourage listening. The activity is designed to help your children develop comprehension of main ideas. You may wish to point to the pictures and have them give the German equivalents. Keep in mind, however, that comprehension of every word is not nearly as important as overall comprehension—understanding the main ideas of the story.

Audio Transcript

Narrator: Now listen to *meine Geschichte* about *den Bauer und die Rübe,* the farmer and the turnip. Follow along and look at the pictures.

Once there was *ein Bauer* who planted *einen Samen*. He said: "*Eine Pflanze* will grow from *diesen Samen* and *die Pflanze* will make a nice meal for *meine Frau* and *meine Tochter* and me." The *Bauer* sprinkled water on the ground where he had planted *den Samen,* and the sun shone, and after a few days, a little *Pflanze* appeared.

Corresponding Page from Children's Activity Book

Diglot Weave
The Farmer and the Turnip

Once there was 👨‍🌾 who planted 🌰. He said: " 🌱 will grow from *diesen* 🌰 and 🌱 will make a nice meal for *meine* 👩 and *meine* 👧 and me." 👨‍🌾 Sprinkled water on the ground where he had planted 🌰 and the sun shone and after a few days, a little 🌿 appeared.

63

Diglot Weave

This is the next section of the multi-page diglot weave narrative of "The Farmer and the Turnip."

Instructions for This Page

Have your children continue to listen carefully and follow the story in their activity books as it is told on the tape.

Audio Transcript

Narrator: And he sprinkled water on the little *Pflanze* and the sun shone, and *die Pflanze* grew and grew. Every day he sprinkled water on *die Pflanze*, and every day the sun shone, and every day *die Pflanze* grew and grew.

After many days *die Pflanze* was very big. And *der Bauer* said: "I think *die Rübe* is ripe." So he took hold of *die Pflanze* and he tried to pull it out... but *die Rübe* didn't come out.

Corresponding Page from Children's Activity Book

And he sprinkled water on the little 🌱 and the sun shone, and 🌱 grew and grew. Every day he sprinkled water on 🌱, and every day the sun shone, and every day 🌱 grew and grew.

After many days 🌱 was very big.

And 👨 said: "I think 🌰 is ripe."

So he took hold of 🌱 and he tried to pull it out... but 🌰 didn't come out.

64

Diglot Weave

This is the next section of the multi-page diglot weave narrative of "The Farmer and the Turnip."

Instructions for This Page

Have your children continue to listen carefully and follow the story in their activity books as it is told on the tape.

Audio Transcript

Narrator: So the *Bauer* called his *Frau*: "*Frau*, come here. *Frau*, come and help me." And so his *Frau* came to help. She took hold of *den Bauer* and *der Bauer* took hold of *die Pflanze* and they pulled and pulled... but *die Rübe* didn't come out.

So *der Bauer* called his *Tochter*: "*Tochter*, come here. *Tochter*, come and help us." And so *die Tochter* came to help.

Corresponding Page from Children's Activity Book

So 🧑‍🌾 called his 👤: "👤, come here. 👤, come and help me." And so 👤 came to help. She took hold of 🧑‍🌾 and 🧑‍🌾 took hold of 🌱 and they pulled and pulled... but 🌱 didn't come out.

So 🧑‍🌾 called his 👧: "👧, come here. 👧, come and help us." And so 👧 came to help.

65

Diglot Weave

This is the next section of the multi-page diglot weave narrative of "The Farmer and the Turnip."

Instructions for This Page

Have your children continue to listen carefully and follow the story in their activity books as it is told on the tape.

Audio Transcript

Narrator: She took hold of *die Frau* and *die Frau* took hold of *den Bauer* and *der Bauer* took hold of *die Pflanze*, and they pulled and pulled… but *die Rübe* didn't come out.

So they called *den Hund*: "*Hund*, come here. Come and help us." So *der Hund* came to help.

Corresponding Page from Children's Activity Book

She took hold of 👤 and 👤 took hold of 👨‍🌾 and 👨‍🌾 took hold of 🌱, and they pulled and pulled… but 🥕 didn't come out.

So they called 🐕 : "🐕, come here. Come and help us." So 🐕 came to help.

66

Diglot Weave

This is the next section of the multi-page diglot weave narrative of "The Farmer and the Turnip."

Instructions for This Page

Have your children continue to listen carefully and follow the story in their activity books as it is told on the tape.

Audio Transcript

Narrator: *Der Hund* took hold of *die Tochter und die Tochter* took hold of *die Frau und die Frau* took hold of *den Bauer* and *der Bauer* took hold of *die Pflanze* and they pulled and pulled... but *die Rübe* didn't come out.

So the *Bauer* called *die Katze*: "*Katze*, come here *Katze*. Come and help us." So *die Katze* came to help.

Corresponding Page from Children's Activity Book

🐱 took hold of 👧 und 👧 took hold of 👩 und 👩 took hold of 👨 and 👨 took hold of 🌱 and they pulled and pulled... but 🌱 didn't come out.

So 👨 called 🐱: "🐱, come here 🐱. Come and help us." So 🐱 came to help.

67

Diglot Weave

This is the next section of the multi-page diglot weave narrative of "The Farmer and the Turnip."

Instructions for This Page

Have your children continue to listen carefully and follow the story in their activity books as it is told on the tape.

Audio Transcript

Narrator: *Die Katze* took hold of *den Hund und der Hund* took hold of *die Tochter und die Tochter* took hold of *die Frau und die Frau* took hold of *den Bauer und der Bauer* took hold of *die Pflanze*, and they pulled and they pulled… but *die Rübe* didn't come out.

At that moment, a little mouse, a little *Maus,* came by and *die Maus* said: "Hey, what's going on here?"

Corresponding Page from Children's Activity Book

🐱 took hold of 🐶 und 🐶 took hold of 👧 und 👧 took hold of 👩 und 👩 took hold of 👨 und 👨 took hold of 🌱, and they pulled and they pulled… but 🥕 didn't come out.

At that moment, a little mouse, a little 🐭 came by and 🐭 said: "Hey, what's going on here?"

68

Diglot Weave

This is the next section of the multi-page diglot weave narrative of "The Farmer and the Turnip."

Instructions for This Page

Have your children continue to listen carefully and follow the story in their activity books as it is told on the tape.

Audio Transcript

Narrator: And the *Bauer* explained: "We pull and we pull, but *die Rübe* won't come out." Then the little *Maus* said: "Maybe I can help." At first they all laughed at him: "Ha ha ha ha. You're so little. How can you help us?" But *die Maus* said: "Well, we can all at least try one more time."

Corresponding Page from Children's Activity Book

And 🐛 explained: "We pull and we pull, but 🌱 won't come out." Then the little 🐭 said: "Maybe I can help." At first they all laughed at him: "Ha ha ha ha. You're so little. How can you help us?" But 🐭 said: "Well, we can all at least try one more time."

69

Diglot Weave

This is the next section of the multi-page diglot weave narrative of "The Farmer and the Turnip."

Instructions for This Page

Have your children continue to listen carefully and follow the story in their activity books as it is told on the tape.

Audio Transcript

Narrator: And so *die Maus* took hold of *die Katze, und die Katze* took hold of *der Hund, und der Hund* took hold of *die Tochter, und die Tochter* took hold of *die Frau, und die Frau* took hold of *der Bauer, und der Bauer* took hold of *die Pflanze, und* they pulled *und* they pulled *und*... guess what happened? *Die Rübe* came out.

Corresponding Page from Children's Activity Book

And so 🐭 took hold of 🐱, *und* 🐱 took hold of 🐶, *und* 🐶 took hold of 👧, *und* 👧 took hold of 👩, *und* 👩 took hold of 👨, *und* 👨 took hold of 🌱, *und* they pulled *und* they pulled *und*... guess what happened? 🌰 came out.

70

Diglot Weave

This is the last section of the multi-page diglot weave narrative about "The Farmer and the Turnip."

Instructions for This Page

Have your children continue to listen carefully and follow the story in their activity books as it is told on the tape.

Audio Transcript

Narrator: Just think, from that tiny little *Samen* that *der Bauer* planted, with plenty of water *und* plenty of sun, a big *Pflanze* and a giant *Rübe* grew. *Und* for ten days *die Maus, und die Katze, und der Hund, und die Tochter, und die Frau, und der Bauer* ate *die Rübe*. Nothing remained save one tiny little *Samen*.

Corresponding Page from Children's Activity Book

Just think, from that tiny little 🌰 that 👨‍🌾 planted, with plenty of water *und* plenty of sun, a big 🌱 and a giant 🥕 grew. *Und* for ten days 🐭, *und* 🐱, *und* 🐕, *und* 👧, *und* 👩, *und* 👨‍🌾 ate 🥕. Nothing remained save one tiny little 🌰.

71

Match and Learn

This activity uses frames once again to introduce some new pictures that can then be incorporated into the telling of the story.

Instructions for This Page

Have your children point to the correct pictures as the tape instructs. Have your children pause the tape as needed to have time to give their answers.

Have your children come up with frames of their own! These can then be used as flashcards.

Audio Transcript

Narrator: Here are a few more pictures and new words to learn.

Look at frame 1. Point to *die Sonne*. It is in the top white box, right? Yes. Now point to *der Bauer gießt,* waters, the seed. It is in the bottom white box, right? No, it is in the bottom gray box. Point to *der Bauer gießt die Pflanze.* Is "the farmer waters the plant" in the bottom white box? Yes, it is. Now point to *die Maus.* The *Maus* is in the top gray box, right? Yes.

Now look at frame 2. Point to *der Bauer* pulls, *zieht, die Rübe.* The *Bauer zient die Rübe.* It is in the top white box, right? No, it is in the bottom white box. Now point to *die Katze zient* the *Maus.* "The cat pulls the mouse." It's in the bottom gray box, right? Yes. Point to the farmer, *der Bauer,* takes hold of, *griff nach,* his wife—*seiner Frau.* "*Der Bauer griff nach seiner Frau.*" That's in the top white box, right? Now point to *die Frau griff nach dem Bauer.* The wife takes hold of the farmer. That is in the top white box, right? No, it is in the top gray box.

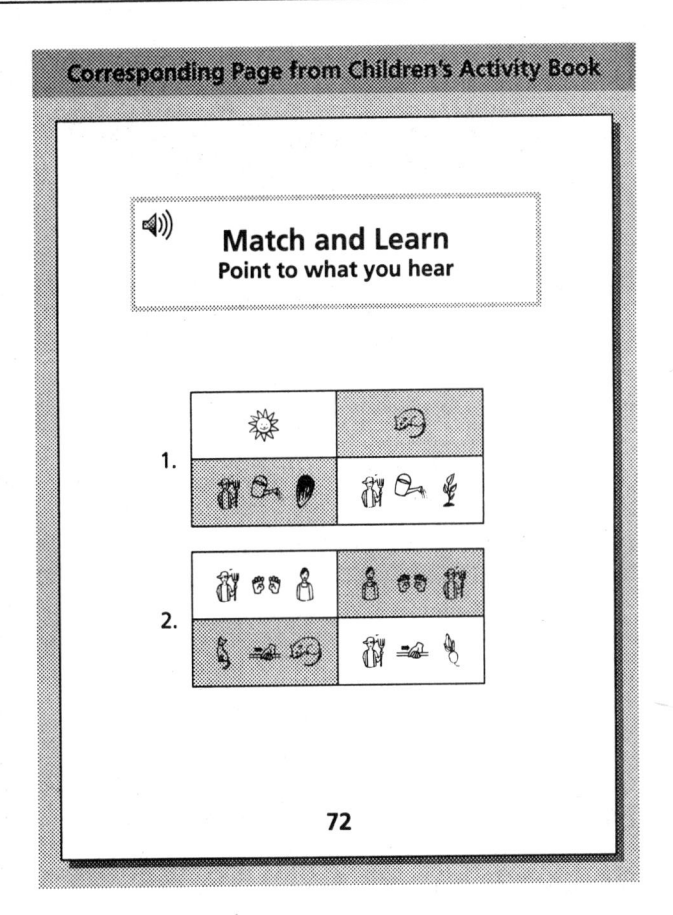

The Farmer and the Turnip | P–89 | Match and Learn

Describe What You See

This activity requires your children to use the German words they learned in the previous activities to describe the pictures they see.

Instructions for This Page

Have your children say the German words for the pictures, or write them on the blank lines to the side of the pictures.

Have your children say or write in as many of the German words as they can on their own. Then you may go back through with them and help them remember those they missed. Continue to encourage them to guess when they need to, and to not feel bad when they cannot remember all the words or when they get one wrong.

Audio Transcript

Narrator: On this page are some of the pictures you have learned the words for. Say the German words for the pictures. Or if you like, write the German words for the pictures in the blanks.

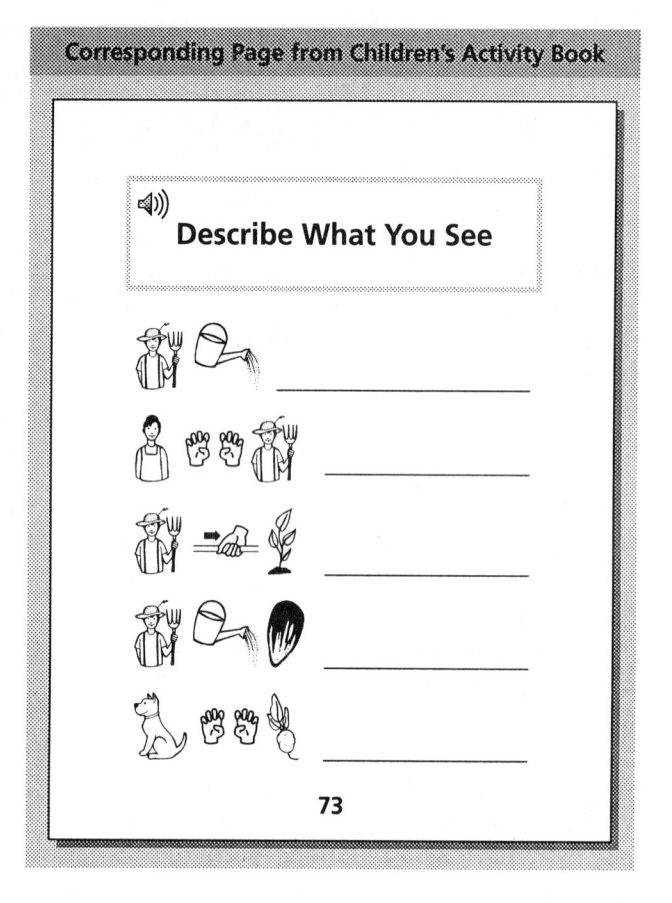

Corresponding Page from Children's Activity Book

Describe What You See

The Farmer and the Turnip

Story Telling

This activity lets your children use the German words they have learned to tell the story of "The Farmer and the Turnip" themselves. The story extends for three pages.

Instructions for This Page

Have your children follow the trail of pictures (from top to bottom) with their finger, telling the story using the German words for the pictured items as they go. The diagonal lines set off sections of the story.

If your children cannot remember a particular word let them think for a moment, and then go ahead and help them. Your goal here is to encourage them to think as hard as they can on their own, while keeping them from getting discouraged. Encourage them to create their own stories if they like, using the pictures in this activity.

Audio Transcript

Narrator: Now it's your turn to tell the story. Follow the trail of pictures from top to bottom with your finger, telling the story using as many German words as you can. The pictures will remind you how the story goes, and don't worry when you have to put in some English.

Story Telling

This is a continuation of the story of "The Farmer and a Turnip."

Instructions for This Page

Have your children follow the trail of pictures (from top to bottom) with their finger, telling the story using the German words for the pictured items as they go.

If your children cannot remember a particular word let them think for a moment, and then go ahead and help them. Your goal here is to encourage them to think as much as they can on their own, while keeping them from getting discouraged. Encourage them to create their own stories using the pictures in this activity.

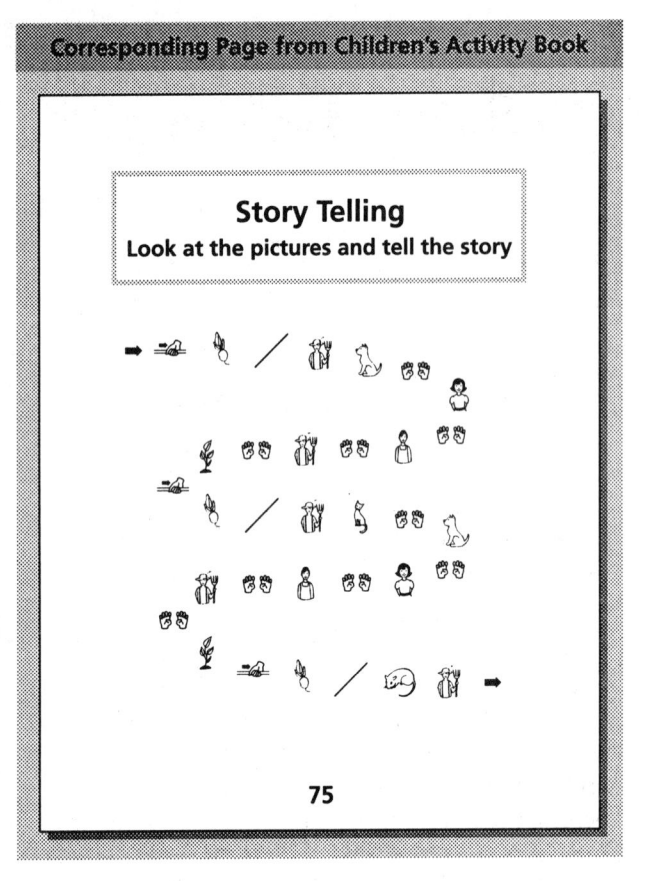

Corresponding Page from Children's Activity Book

Story Telling
Look at the pictures and tell the story

75

Story Telling

This is a continuation of the story of "The Farmer and a Turnip."

Instructions for This Page

Have your children follow the trail of pictures (from top to bottom) with their finger, telling the story using the German words for the pictured items as they go.

💡 If your children cannot remember a particular word let them think for a moment, and then go ahead and help them. Your goal here is to encourage them to think as hard as they can on their own, while keeping them from getting frustrated or discouraged. Encourage them to create their own stories using the pictures in this activity.

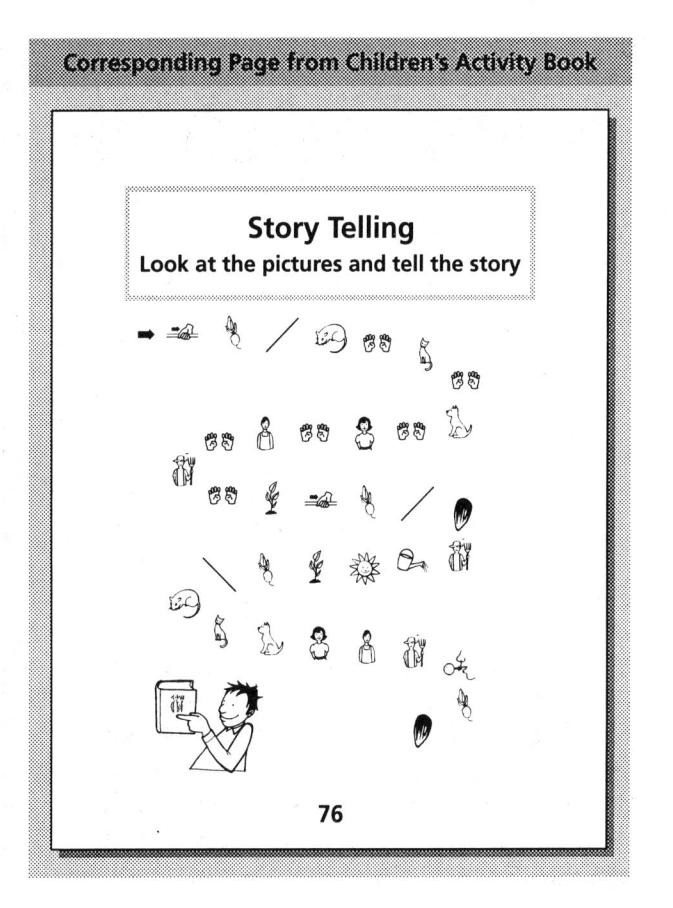

Corresponding Page from Children's Activity Book

Story Telling
Look at the pictures and tell the story

Practice in German

This activity asks your children to tell the story of "The Farmer and the Turnip" themselves using the pictures from the story (contained in the big circle in their activity books) as memory prompts.

Instructions for This Page

Have your children point to the pictures in the circle in their activity books as they tell the story of "The Farmer and the Turnip" on their own, using the German words they have learned. Record how long it takes them to tell the complete story in German their first time, and then record their best time on a third or fourth trial run.

> 💡 If necessary, review the story with your children, using the audio transcript provided in this *Parent's Guide*.

Audio Transcript

🔊 Narrator: Now that you have reviewed the story, see how much of it you can tell by yourself. All the pictures used in the story are in the big circle on your workbook page. Point to the pictures in the right order as you tell the story. Turn the tape off as you tell the story, and turn it on again when you finish.

Were you able to tell the whole story on your own, with mostly German words?

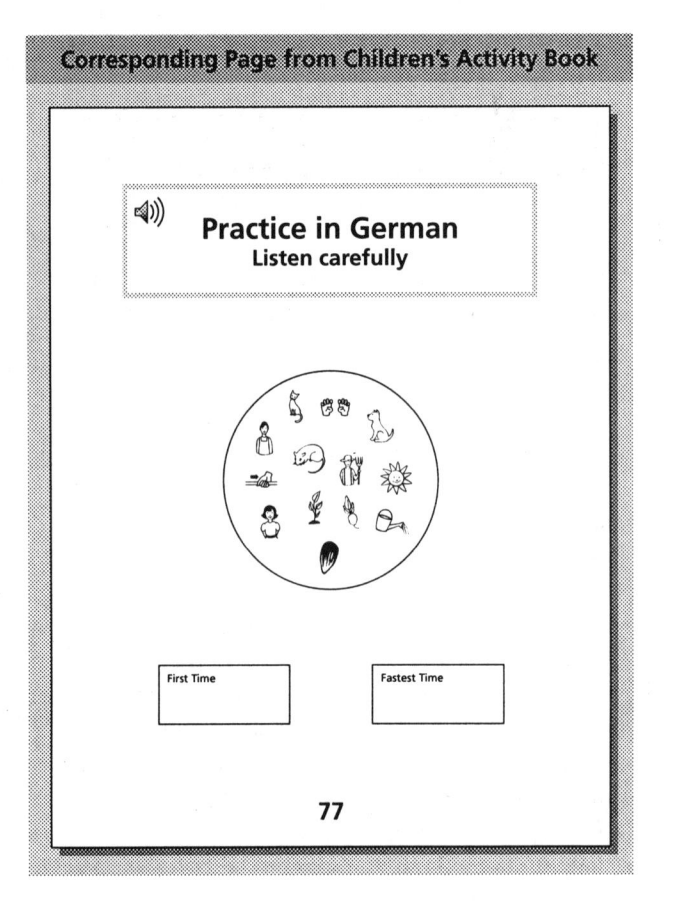

Hungry Hunters Head Home

This section contains an audio transcript of the adventure story your children will hear on the tape.

Instructions for This Page

Have your children listen carefully as the adventure story is read on the tape.

Encourage your children to take an active part in listening to the adventure story. Ask them to respond to things they hear and have them say out loud words said by the characters on the tape. Younger children might enjoy coloring the picture as the adventure story is read. Older children may want to follow along with the written audio transcript provided in this *Parent's Guide*.

Audio Transcript

Narrator 2: The Adventure Continues: Hungry Hunters Head Home

Serena: I really liked that story, Dieter. It must have been a really huge turnip to take all those people and animals to pull it out. It must have been even bigger than these yams!

Dieter: Yes. It must have been. And now, my friends, it's getting on in the afternoon. I think you had better wait until tomorrow to try to cross the lake to the island. The treasure you're hunting for there will have to wait until tomorrow. You see, the ferry only goes back and forth in the morning and the late afternoon, so if you went now you'd have to spend the night there.

Max: I guess you're right, Dieter. We'll go tomorrow. After all, the spot on the island is the second to last one, and we don't have to leave until the day after tomorrow.

Narrator: "And," you add, "I'm starving after harvesting these yams all day!"

Dieter: Me too. Let's head home and see what Nicole has prepared for dinner!

Narrator: An hour later you arrive back at the mill house.

Nicole: *Hallo*, everyone one! I hope you're hungry—I thought you would be after harvesting all day, so I've cooked a dinner a giant would enjoy. Come in!

Narrator: You all sit around Nicole and Dieter's table, and as you eat Dieter offers to tell you another story, this time one about a hungry giant.

A Hungry Giant

It is important for children to first understand spoken language, but it is more exciting when they begin to use it, and that is where the learning really takes off.

In this activity we continue with comprehension building, but as the activities progress, we gradually introduce conversation.

Your children will hear a story about a hungry giant several times. They will learn the character names and identify them with pictures. By the time we get to their telling the story, they will have learned to recognize the pictures well enough that they can pretty much tell the story simply by looking at the pictures.

Instructions for This Page

Have your children look at the first page of the story "A Hungry Giant" and listen to the introduction to the story on the tape.

Audio Transcript

Narrator 2: Activity: A Hungry Giant.

Narrator: This is the story of "A Hungry Giant."

Match and Learn

This activity is visual, audio, and kinesthetic. It is designed to help your children learn by listening and pointing.

Instructions for This Page

Have your children point to the correct boxes and pictures as the tape instructs. In the second part of the activity have them answer out loud the questions asked about the numbered pictures. The purpose of this activity is simply to teach the system of frames and numbered pictures in preparation for German learning using these tools in subsequent sections.

Have your children pause the tape as needed to have time to give their answers.

Corresponding Page from Children's Activity Book

Match and Learn
Point to what you hear

Audio Transcript

Narrator: Before I tell you this *Geschichte*, I'll teach you some new words to help you understand.

Look at frame 1. Point to the giant, the *Riese*. The *Riese* is in the top white box, right? Now point to the crocodile, the *Krokodil*. The *Krokodil* is in the bottom gray box, right? Now point to the fly, the *Fliege*. Is the *Fliege* in the top gray box? No, the *Fliege* is in the bottom white box, right? Now point to the spider, the *Spinne*. It is in the top gray box, right?

Now look at frame 2. Point to the *Spinne*. It is in the bottom white box, right? Now point to the *Krokodil*. He is in the top white box, right? Now point to the *Riese*. It is in the bottom gray box, right? Now point to the *Vogel*, the bird. It is in the top gray box, right?

Now look at frame 3. Point to the *Vogel*. It is in the top gray box, right? No, the *Vogel* is in the bottom gray box. Now point to the whale, the *Wal*. It is in the top gray box, right? Now point to the *Katze*, the cat. It is in the top white box, isn't it? Yes. Now point to the *Krokodil*. It is in the bottom gray box, right? No, it is in the bottom white box.

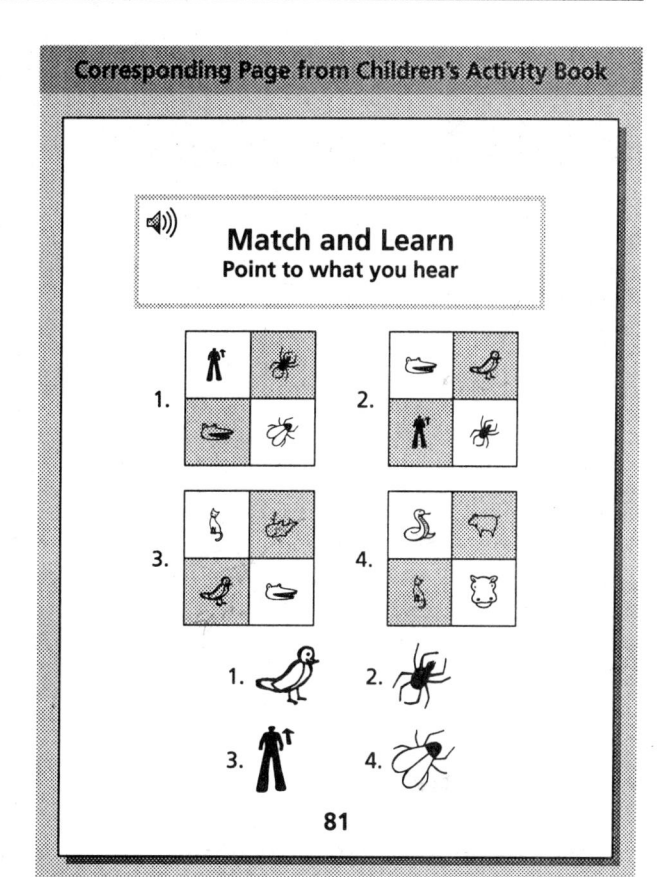

Now look at frame 4. Point to the hippopotamus, the *Nilpferd*. The *Nilpferd* is in the bottom white box, right? Yes. Now point to the *Schwein*, the pig. The *Schwein* is in the top gray box, right? Now point to the *Schlange*, the snake. The *Schlange* is in the bottom gray box, right? No, the *Schlange* is in the top white box. Now point to the *Katze*. The *Katze* is in the bottom gray box, right?

Now see if you can answer some questions about the words you just learned. Look at the picture with the number one next to it.

Number 1. Is this a *Vogel*? Yes, this is a *Vogel*.

Number 2. Is this a *Spinne*? Yes, this is a *Spinne*.

Number 3. Is this a *Riese* or a *Fliege*? Did you say a giant, a *Riese*? Yes, this is a *Riese*.

Number 4. Is this a *Spinne*? No, this is a *Fliege*.

Match and Learn

This activity uses frames once again to introduce some new pictures and words that can then be incorporated into the telling of the story.

Instructions for This Page

Have your children point to the correct pictures as the tape instructs. In the second part of the activity have them answer out loud the questions asked about the numbered pictures.

As these activities become progressively more challenging, the main objective is to help your children feel confident. They should not be overly concerned with correctness. Encourage them to point boldly as soon as they hear what to point to in the first part of the activity, and to speak out loud in response to the questions in the second half. When your children guess wrong, let them know it's okay and to keep making their best guesses.

Audio Transcript

Narrator: Did you do well with those pictures and words? Good. Let's try a few more.

Look at frame 5. Point to the *Leopard*. The *Leopard*, the leopard, is in the top gray box, right? Now point to the *Riese*. The *Riese* is in the bottom white box, right? No, it is in the bottom gray box. Now point to the *Fliege*. The *Fliege* is in the bottom white box, right? Yes. Now point to the *Krokodil*. It's in the top white box, right? Yes!

Now look at frame 6. Point to the *Leopard und* the *Fliege*. They are in the top gray box, right? Yes. Now point to the *Krokodil und* the *Wal*. They are in the bottom gray box, right? No, they are in the top white box. Point to the *Vogel und* the *Krokodil*. The *Vogel und* the *Krokodil* are in the bottom gray box, right? Yes. Now point to the *Schlange* and the *Schwein*. The *Schlange und* the *Schwein* are in the bottom white box, right?

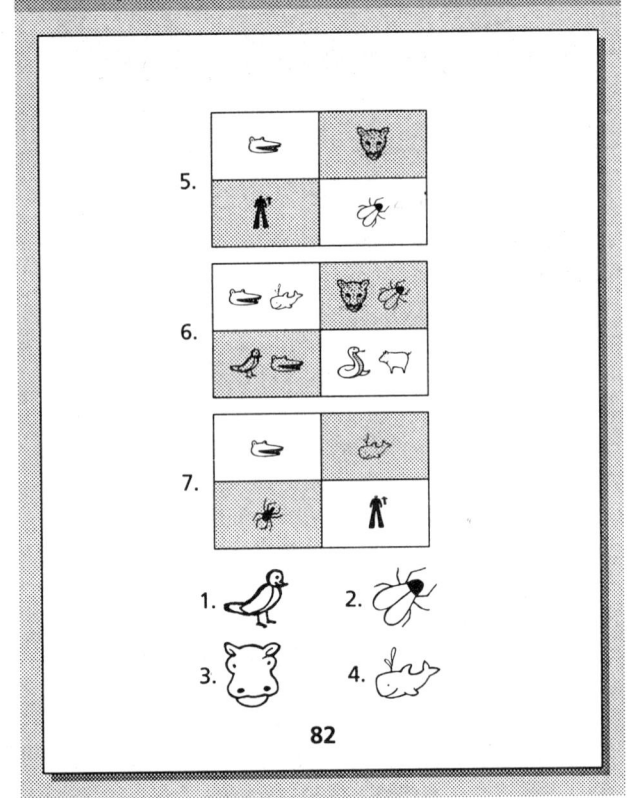

Now look at frame 7. Point to the *Riese*. The *Riese* is in the bottom white box, right? Yes. He is. Now point to the *Wal*. It is in the top gray box, right? Yes. Now point to the *Spinne*. Is it in the bottom white box? No, it is in the bottom gray box. Now point to the *Krokodil*. It's in the top white box, right? Yes.

Now, see if you can answer some questions about the words you just learned.

Look at picture number 1. Is this a *Vogel*? Yes, this is a *Vogel*.

Picture number 2. Is this a *Krokodil* or a *Fliege*? It is a *Fliege*.

Picture number 3. Is this a *Wal*? No, this is a *Nilpferd*.

Picture number 4 is a *Krokodil*, right? No, it is a *Wal*.

Match and Learn

This activity uses frames once again to introduce some new pictures that can then be incorporated into the telling of the story.

Instructions for This Page

Have your children point to the correct pictures as the tape instructs. Have your children pause the tape as needed to have time to give their answers.

💡 Have your children come up with frames of their own! These can then be used as flashcards.

Audio Transcript

🔊 Narrator: Here are a few more pictures and new words to learn.

Look at frame 1. Point to the *Schlange*. It is in the top white box, right? Yes. Now point to the *Krokodil fraß die Spinne*, the crocodile ate the spider. It is in the bottom gray box, right? Yes. Now point to the *Wal fraß das Krokodil*. Is "the whale ate the crocodile" in the bottom white box? Yes, it is. Now point to the boy likes, *der Junge mag*. *Der Junge mag* is in the top gray box.

Now look at frame 2. Point to *Mann dachte*, "man thought." *Mann dachte* is in the top white box, right? Yes. Now point to the *Katze dachte*. Can you guess what this means? That's right! It means, "cat thought." It's in the bottom gray box, right? Yes. Now point to the *Krokodil fraß den Vogel*. That's in the bottom white box, right? Now point to *der Junge mag keine*. That is in the bottom gray box, right? No, it is in the top gray box. *Der Junge mag keine* means "the boy does not like."

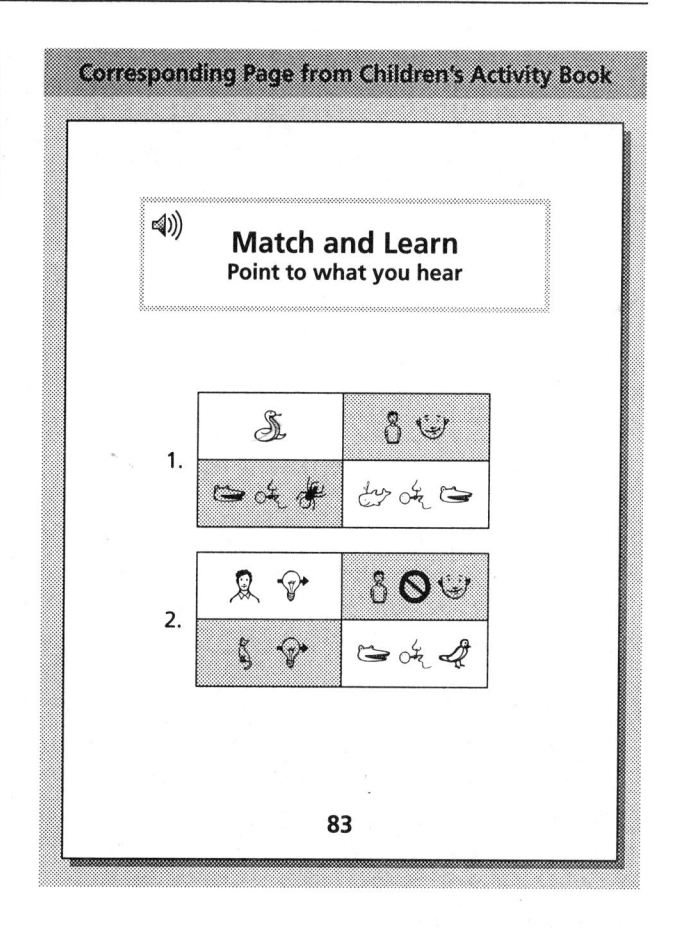

Corresponding Page from Children's Activity Book

🔊 **Match and Learn**
Point to what you hear

83

Describe What You See

This activity requires your children to use the German words they learned in the previous activities to describe the pictures they see.

Instructions for This Page

Have your children say the German words for the pictures, or write them on the blank lines to the side of the pictures.

Have your children say or write in as many of the German words as they can on their own. Then you may go back through with them and help them remember those they missed. Continue to encourage them to guess when they need to, and to not feel bad when they cannot remember all the words or when they get one wrong.

Audio Transcript

Narrator: On this page are some of the pictures you have learned the words for. Say the German words for the pictures. Or if you like, write the German words for the pictures in the blanks.

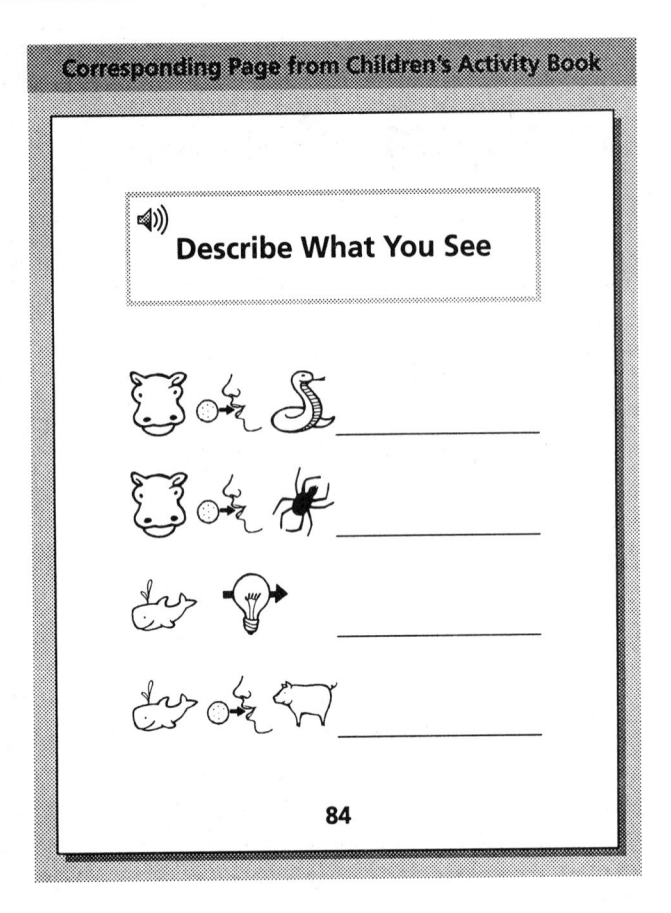

Diglot Weave

The following multi-page activity contains an extended diglot weave narrative built around the words from the previous activities.

Instructions for This Page

Have your children listen carefully and follow the story in their activity books as it is told on the tape.

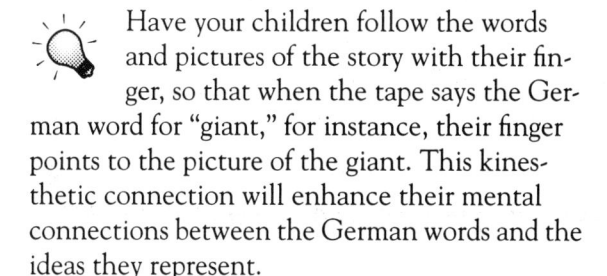

Have your children follow the words and pictures of the story with their finger, so that when the tape says the German word for "giant," for instance, their finger points to the picture of the giant. This kinesthetic connection will enhance their mental connections between the German words and the ideas they represent.

If the pace is ever too fast, stop the tape and review with your children. Be sure to reward understanding and encourage listening. The activity is designed to help your children develop comprehension of main ideas. You may wish to point to the pictures and have them give the German equivalents. Keep in mind, however, that comprehension of every word is not nearly as important as overall comprehension—understanding the main ideas of the story.

Audio Transcript

Narrator: Now listen to the story of "A Hungry Giant." Follow along and look at the pictures.

Have you ever seen a *Riesen*? Do you know how big a *Riese* is? *Weißt du* how much a *Riese* can eat? I haven't ever seen a *Reisen*, but one time my father (*mein Vater*) saw one. Anyway *mein Vater* told me he saw one. This happened when he was just *ein Junge* your age.

Corresponding Page from Children's Activity Book

Diglot Weave
A Hungry Giant

Have you ever seen a *Riesen*? Do you know how big a *Riese* is? *Weißt du* how much a *Riese* can eat? I haven't ever seen a *Reisen*, but one time my father (*mein Vater*) saw one. Anyway *mein Vater* told me he saw one. This happened when he was just *ein Junge* your age.

85

Diglot Weave

This is the next section of the multi-page diglot weave narrative of "A Hungry Giant."

Instructions for This Page

Have your children continue to listen carefully and follow the story in their activity books as it is told on the tape.

Audio Transcript

Narrator: One morning before breakfast he took a walk and saw *eine Fliege* that was caught in a spider's web. He watched *die Spinne* come and eat the fly.

Gut! ("Good!") thought *mein Vater.* "*Die Spinne* has eaten *die Fliege*. I don't like flies... *Ich mag keine Fliegen.*"

Corresponding Page from Children's Activity Book

One morning before breakfast he took a walk and saw *eine Fliege* that was caught in a spider's web. He watched *die Spinne* come and eat the fly.

Gut! ("Good!") thought *mein Vater.* "*Die Spinne* has eaten *die Fliege*. I don't like flies . . . *Ich mag keine Fliegen.*"

Diglot Weave

This is the next section of the multi-page diglot weave narrative of "A Hungry Giant."

Instructions for This Page

Have your children continue to listen carefully and follow the story in their activity books as it is told on the tape.

Audio Transcript

Narrator: A moment later, a *Vogel* came and *fraß die Spinne*. "*Gut,*" thought *mein Vater*. "*Der Vogel* has eaten *die Spinne. Ich mag keine Spinnen.*"

The next moment *eine Katze* came along *und fraß den Vogel. Und mein Vater dachte*: "Too bad; *Ich mag Vögel.*"

Corresponding Page from Children's Activity Book

A moment later, a *Vogel* came and *fraß die Spinne*. "*Gut,*" thought *mein Vater*. "*Der Vogel* has eaten *die Spinne. Ich mag keine Spinnen.*"

The next moment *eine Katze* came along *und fraß den Vogel. Und mein Vater dachte*: "Too bad; *Ich mag Vögel.*"

87

Diglot Weave

This is the next section of the multi-page diglot weave narrative of "A Hungry Giant."

Instructions for This Page

Have your children continue to listen carefully and follow the story in their activity books as it is told on the tape.

Audio Transcript

Narrator: The next moment *eine Schlange* came along *und fraß die Katze. Und mein Vater dachte:* "Too bad, *ich mag Katzen.*"

The next moment *ein Schwein* came along *und fraß die Schlange. Und mein Vater dachte:* "Gut, *das Schwein* has eaten *die Schlange. Ich mag keine Schlangen.*"

Corresponding Page from Children's Activity Book

The next moment *eine Schlange* came along *und fraß die Katze. Und mein Vater dachte:* "Too bad, *ich mag Katzen.*"

The next moment *ein Schwein* came along *und fraß die Schlange. Und mein Vater dachte:* "Gut, *das Schwein* has eaten *die Schlange. Ich mag keine Schlangen.*"

Diglot Weave

This is the next section of the multi-page diglot weave narrative of "A Hungry Giant."

Instructions for This Page

Have your children continue to listen carefully and follow the story in their activity books as it is told on the tape.

Audio Transcript

Narrator: Before long *ein Leopard* came along *und fraß das Schwein. Und mein Vater dachte:* "Gut, *ein Leopard* has eaten *das Schwein.* This is exciting!"

A while later *ein Krokodil* came along *und fraß den Leopard. Und mein Vater dachte:* "Wow, *ein Krokodil* has eaten *den Leopard.* This is really exciting. What will happen now?"

Corresponding Page from Children's Activity Book

Before long *ein Leopard* came along *und fraß das Schwein. Und mein Vater dachte:* "Gut, *ein Leopard* has eaten *das Schwein.* This is exciting!"

A while later *ein Krokodil* came along *und fraß den Leopard. Und mein Vater dachte:* "Wow, *ein Krokodil* has eaten *den Leopard.* This is really exciting. What will happen now?"

Diglot Weave

This is the next section of the multi-page diglot weave narrative of "A Hungry Giant."

Instructions for This Page

Have your children continue to listen carefully and follow the story in their activity books as it is told on the tape.

Audio Transcript

Narrator: Before long *ein Nilpferd* came along *und fraß das Krokodil. Und mein Vater dachte:* "Wow, *ein Nilpferd* has eaten *das Krokodil.* What will happen now?"

A moment later *ein Wal* came along *und fraß das Nilpferd. Und mein Vater dachte:* "Wow, this is too much."

Corresponding Page from Children's Activity Book

Before long *ein Nilpferd* came along *und fraß das Krokodil. Und mein Vater dachte:* "Wow, *ein Nilpferd* has eaten *das Krokodil.* What will happen now?"

A moment later *ein Wal* came along *und fraß das Nilpferd. Und mein Vater dachte:* "Wow, this is too much."

90

Diglot Weave

This is the next section of the multi-page diglot weave narrative of "A Hungry Giant."

Instructions for This Page

Have your children continue to listen carefully and follow the story in their activity books as it is told on the tape.

Audio Transcript

Narrator: "Just imagine: *Ein Wal* has eaten *ein Nilpferd, das Nilpferd* has eaten *ein Krokodil, das Krokodil* has eaten *einen Leopard, der Leopard* has eaten *ein Schwein, das Schwein* has eaten *eine Schlange, die Schlange* has eaten *eine Katze, die Katze* has eaten *einen Vogel, der Vogel* has eaten *eine Spinne, und die Spinne* has eaten *eine Fliege.* That's amazing! I've never seen such a thing."

Corresponding Page from Children's Activity Book

"Just imagine: *Ein Wal* has eaten *ein Nilpferd, das Nilpferd* has eaten *ein Krokodil, das Krokodil* has eaten *einen Leopard, der Leopard* has eaten *ein Schwein, das Schwein* has eaten *eine Schlange, die Schlange* has eaten *eine Katze, die Katze* has eaten *einen Vogel, der Vogel* has eaten *eine Spinne, und die Spinne* has eaten *eine Fliege.* That's amazing! I've never seen such a thing."

Diglot Weave

This is the next section of the multi-page diglot weave narrative of "A Hungry Giant."

Instructions for This Page

Have your children continue to listen carefully and follow the story in their activity books as it is told on the tape.

Audio Transcript

Narrator: Just then *eine Hand* reached down from the sky and picked up the whale. *Mein Vater* looked up just as *der Riese* swallowed the whole whale. And he thought: "Wow, this is the first time I've seen a giant."

Maybe he's still hungry (*hungrig*). I'd better get out of here!" And he ran home as fast as he could.

Corresponding Page from Children's Activity Book

Just then *eine Hand* reached down from the sky and picked up the whale. *Mein Vater* looked up just as *der Riese* swallowed the whole whale. And he thought: "Wow, this is the first time I've seen a giant.

Maybe he's still hungry (*hungrig*). I'd better get out of here!" And he ran home as fast as he could.

92

Diglot Weave

This is the last section of the multi-page diglot weave narrative about "A Hungry Giant."

Instructions for This Page

Have your children continue to listen carefully and follow the story in their activity books as it is told on the tape.

Audio Transcript

Narrator: And there, as he ate a big bowl of mush, he thought of *die Fliege und die Spinne und den Vogel und die Katze und die Schlange und das Schwein und den Leopard und das Krokodil und das Nilpherd und den Wal.*

Aber most of all he thought of *den Riesen, und wie hungrig* he must have been.

Corresponding Page from Children's Activity Book

And there, as he ate a big bowl of mush, he thought of *die Fliege und die Spinne und den Vogel und die Katze und die Schlange und das Schwein und den Leopard und das Krokodil und das Nilpherd und den Wal.*

Aber most of all he thought of *den Riesen, und wie hungrig* he must have been.

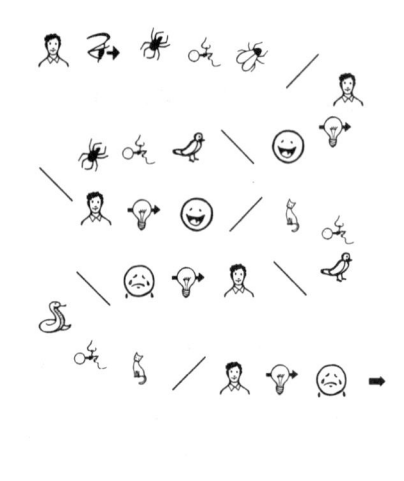

Story Telling

This activity lets your children use the German words they have learned to tell the story of "A Hungry Giant" themselves. The story extends for three pages.

Instructions for This Page

Have your children follow the trail of pictures (from top to bottom) with their finger, telling the story using the German words for the pictured items as they go. The diagonal lines set off sections of the story.

If your children cannot remember a particular word let them think for a moment, and then go ahead and help them. Your goal here is to encourage them to think as hard as they can on their own, while keeping them from getting discouraged.

Two pictographs are used in this story that your children have not seen for a while: the happy face, and crying face, meaning, "happy" or "laugh", and "sad", or "cry". Without reminding your children ahead of time, see if they recognize the faces. Encourage them to create their own stories if they like, using the pictures in this activity.

Audio Transcript

Narrator: Now it's your turn to tell the story. Follow the trail of pictures from top to bottom with your finger, telling the story using as many German words as you can. The pictures will remind you how the story goes, and don't worry when you have to put in some English.

Story Telling

This is a continuation of the story of "A Hungry Giant."

Instructions for This Page

Have your children follow the trail of pictures (from top to bottom) with their finger, telling the story using the German words for the pictured items as they go.

💡 If your children cannot remember a particular word let them think for a moment, and then go ahead and help them. Your goal here is to encourage them to think as much as they can on their own, while keeping them from getting discouraged. Encourage them to create their own stories using the pictures in this activity.

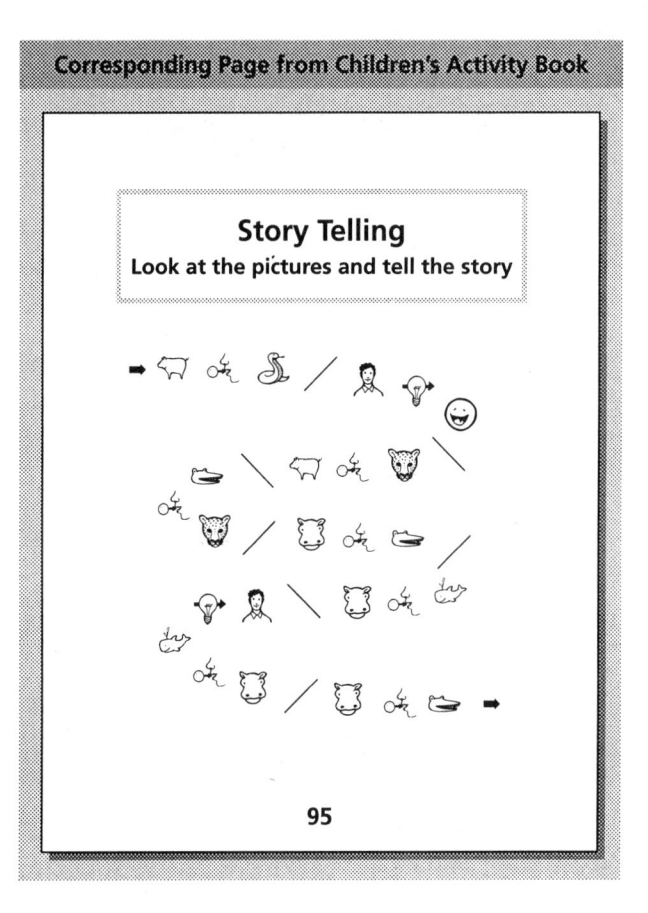

Story Telling

This is a continuation of the story of "A Hungry Giant."

Instructions for This Page

Have your children follow the trail of pictures (from top to bottom) with their finger, telling the story using the German words for the pictured items as they go.

💡 If your children cannot remember a particular word let them think for a moment, and then go ahead and help them. Your goal here is to encourage them to think as hard as they can on their own, while keeping them from getting frustrated or discouraged. Encourage them to create their own stories using the pictures in this activity.

Practice in German

This activity asks your children to tell the story of "A Hungry Giant" themselves using the pictures from the story (contained in the big circle in their activity books) as memory prompts.

Instructions for This Page

Have your children point to the pictures in the circle in their activity books as they tell the story of "A Hungry Giant" on their own, using the German words they have learned. Record how long it takes them to tell the complete story in German their first time, and then record their best time on a third or fourth attempt

💡 If necessary, review the story with your children, using the audio transcript provided in this *Parent's Guide*.

Audio Transcript

🔊 Narrator: Now that you have reviewed the story, see how much of it you can tell by yourself. All the pictures used in the story are in the big circle on your activity book page. Point to the pictures in the right order as you tell the story. Turn the tape off as you tell the story, and turn it on again when you finish.

Were you able to tell the whole story on your own, with mostly German words? Excellent!

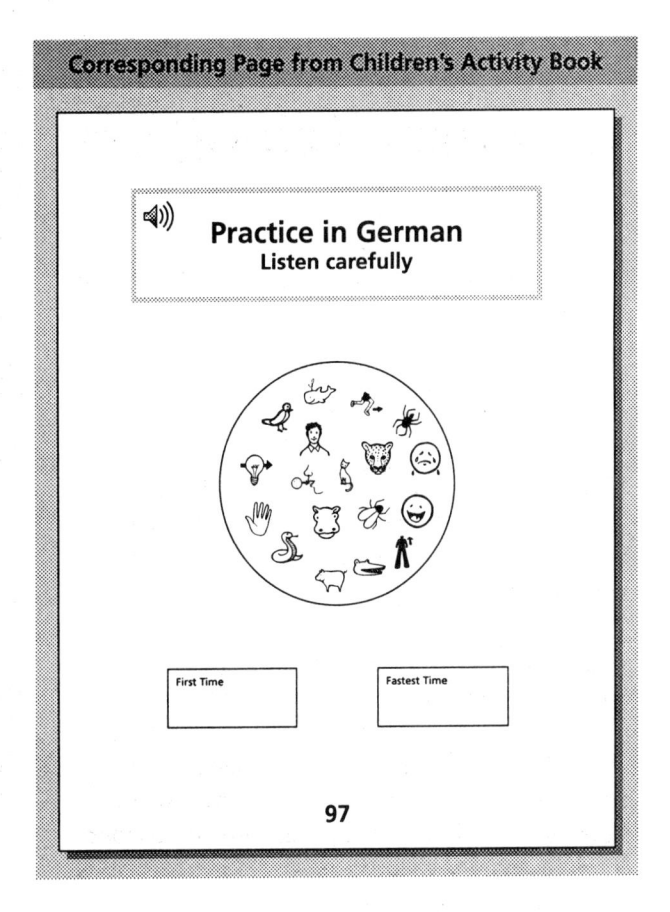

Visiting the Hermit of the Island

This section contains an audio transcript of the adventure story your children will hear on the tape.

Instructions for This Page

Have your children listen carefully as the adventure story is read on the tape. Encourage your children to take an active part in listening to the adventure story. Ask them to respond to things they hear and have them say out loud words said by the characters on the tape.

Younger children might enjoy coloring the picture as the adventure story is read. Older children may want to follow along with the written audio transcript provided in this *Parent's Guide*.

Audio Transcript

Narrator 2: The Adventure Continues: Visiting the Hermit of the Island

Narrator: The next morning, you, Serena and Max make an early start for the lake on the other side of the valley. You go through the village and past the farm where you harvested yams the day before, and eventually reach the lake shore just as a ferry boat is about to cast off.

Max: Hurry, you guys, the boat is about to leave!

Serena: Yeah, and if we miss it, we'll never get the piece of our treasure that's out there.

Narrator: "Wait for us," you yell to the ferry captain as the three of you run along the bank toward the pier. He does, and you all scramble aboard, out of breath, just as the boat casts off. Soon you are cruising steadily across the lake, with you, Max and Serena all leaning against a railing in the front of the boat, enjoying the wind in your faces.

"Wow, this is a beautiful lake," you say, looking over the side.

Serena: I love the deep blue color of the water. I bet it's really deep.

Max: Yeah, it's cool. And I can't wait to get to the island. On the map it doesn't look very big. I wonder who lives there.

Serena: Yeah, me too.

Narrator: The ferry churns along for a while and the island gets closer and closer. "We're almost there now, you guys," you say as the shore gets nearer.

Max: Yeah. Hey, look at that man standing down by the lake shore—over there!

Narrator: Max points to a man standing off to your left, watching the ferry arrive.

Continued from Children's Activity Book, page 99

Serena: Maybe he can help us find the next piece of our treasure. Let's walk down the shore and meet him as soon as we land.

Max: Good idea, Serena.

Narrator: Soon the ferry ride is over and you are all put safely ashore on the little island. The ferry captain reminds you that he will return promptly at 4 o'clock, and then he is gone, leaving the three of you alone on the shore. You begin walking down the shore toward the place where you saw the man. You notice now that this is the same direction your map would have led you anyway, so you're sure you must be getting near the right place. "Hey," you say as you get near the spot you last saw the man, "isn't that the man we saw from the ferry boat?"

Serena: Yeah, it is.

Max: *Guten Tag!*

Herr Einsiedler: *Guten Tag! Ich heiße* Herr Einsiedler. *Kann ich euch helfen?*

Narrator: *"Ja,"* you reply. "We're looking for treasure—*Schatz*. Our *Karte* shows that the next part of the treasure we're looking for is right around here somewhere!"

Herr Einsiedler: Ah, yes. And you are learning German as well, I see.

Max: Yes, we are. Can you help us Herr Einsiedler?

Herr Einsiedler: Yes, I can help you find what you seek. Come into my garden and sit down for a bit, I'll show you what I can.

Serena: Wow, Herr Einsiedler, this is a lovely garden. You must take really good care of it. I don't know if I've ever seen such straight bean rows, or so many flowers with bees buzzing around them.

Herr Einsiedler: My garden is my joy. A well ordered garden reflects a well ordered life, and the bees help everything grow. I have two hives of my own nearby. Now, however, let's get back to your adventure. You have come here in search of treasure, and here you will find some. The piece of your treasure that I have I will only tell you after I show you how it works. To do that, let me tell you a short story.

The Keys to the Gates of Rome

This activity introduces the short story of "The Keys to the Gates of Rome." It teaches comprehension and word identification skills. Your children will first learn some new words, then follow along as a story is told using those new words, and finally tell the story using the familiar pictures as plot prompts.

Instructions for This Page

Have your children look at the picture in their activity book as the story is introduced.

Audio Transcript

Narrator 2: Activity: The Keys to the Gates of Rome.

Narrator: The challenge Herr Einsiedler gave you was to listen to him tell a story using some new German words, and then to tell the story back to him using the new words ourselves. Now let's try together. First, let me introduce the story. It is called "The Keys of the Gates of Rome."

Scatter Chart

This activity uses a Scatter Chart to introduce some new German words that will be used in the story of "The Keys to the Gates of Rome."

Instructions for This Page

Have your children look the pictures on their activity book pages and point to them as the tape directs. Have them say the German words out loud as the tape directs.

Audio Transcript

Narrator: Look at the pictures on your activity book page and point to what you hear.

Point to the *Papagei*. A *Papagei* is a parrot. Say it out loud: *Papagei*. Now point to the *Haus*. A *Haus* is a house. Say it out loud: *Haus*. Now point to the keys. Keys in German are called *Schlüssel*. Say *Schlüssel* out loud: *Schlüssel*. Now point to the *Bett*. Did you point to the bed? Good. Say it out loud: *Bett*. A *Bett* is a bed. Now point to the *Straße*, the road. *Straße* is the German word for road. Say it out loud: *Straße*. Now point to the *Platz*. Did you point to the plaza with trees and a fountain? Good! That is the *Platz*! Say *Platz* out loud: *Platz*. Now, last of all, point to the woman, the *Frau*. *Frau* is a German word for a woman. Say it out loud: *Frau*. Good job!

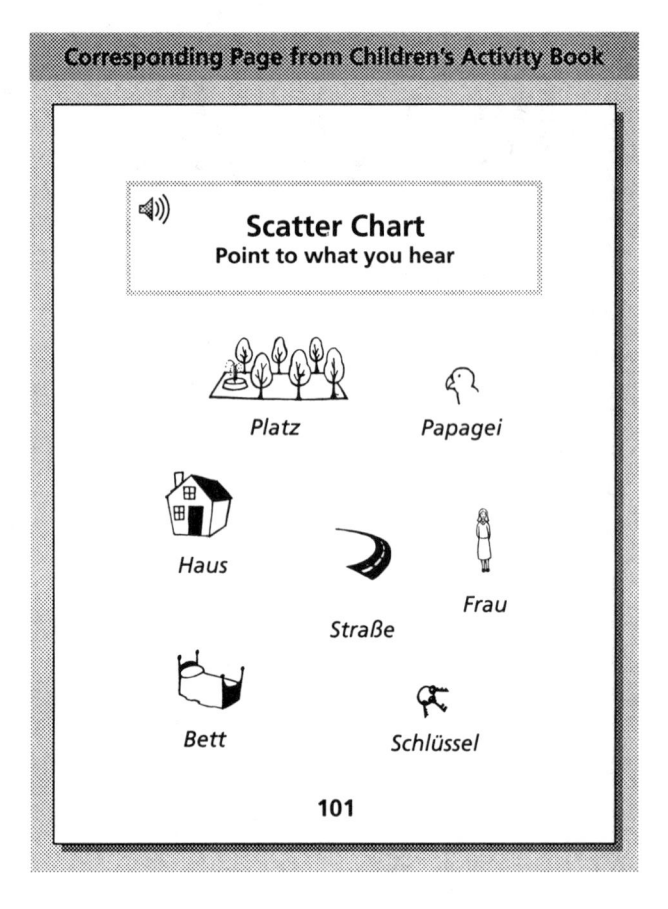

Corresponding Page from Children's Activity Book

Scatter Chart
Point to what you hear

- Platz
- Papagei
- Haus
- Straße
- Frau
- Bett
- Schlüssel

101

Follow Along

This is the story of "The Keys of the Gates of Rome." In your children's activity books only the German words appear, but both the German and English are read on the tape, line by line. The entire story is understandable because translations are given.

Instructions for This Page

Have your children follow along line by line and picture by picture as the story is read on the tape.

Since the next activity asks your children to tell this story on their own using only the pictures, it is important that they learn the story and the words in it well before going on. You may want to have them listen to the entire story two or three times in order to help them become quite familiar with it.

Audio Transcript

Narrator: Here is the story Herr Einsiedler told you. Listen carefully. Follow along line by line, and look at the pictures that go along with the story too. Remember, after you hear the story it will be your turn to tell it, so pay close attention.

These are the Keys of Rome.
Das sind die Schlüssel von Rom.

Take them!
Nimm sie!

In Rome there is a plaza.
In Rom gibt es einen Platz.

In the plaza there is a street.
Auf dem Platz gibt es eine Straße.

In the street there is a house.
Auf der Straße gibt es ein Haus.

Corresponding Page from Children's Activity Book

Follow Along
Point to what you hear

*Das sind die Schlüssel
  von Rom. Nimm sie!
In Rom gibt es einen Platz.
Auf dem Platz gibt es eine Straße.
Auf der Straße gibt es ein Haus.
In dem Haus gibt es ein Bett.
Auf dem Bett gibt es eine Frau.
Bei den Füßen der Frau gibt es einen Papagei.
Und der Papagei sagt: Erzähl keine Lügen!
Die Frau ist nicht auf dem Bett.
Das Bette ist nicht in dem Haus.
Das Haus ist nicht auf der Straße.
Die Straße ist nicht auf dem Platz.
Der Platz ist nicht in Rom.
Und diese Schlüssel sind nicht
  die Schlüssel von Rom.
Verrückter Papagei!*

102

In the house there is a bed.
In dem Haus gibt es ein Bett.

In the bed there is a woman.
Auf dem Bett gibt es eine Frau.

At the woman's feet there is a parrot.
Bei den Füßen der Frau gibt es einen Papagei.

And the parrot says: DON'T LIE!
Und der Papagei sagt: Erzähl keine Lügen!

The woman isn't in the bed.
Die Frau ist nicht auf dem Bett.

The bed isn't in the house.
Das Bette ist nicht in dem Haus.

The house isn't on the street.
Das Haus ist nicht auf der Straße.

The street isn't in the plaza.
Die Straße ist nicht auf dem Platz.

The plaza isn't in Rome.
Der Platz ist nicht in Rom.

Continued from Children's Activity Book, page 102

And these are not the keys of Rome!"
Und diese Schlüssel sind nicht die Schlüssel von Rom.

Crazy parrot!
Verrückter Papagei!

Now again, German only.

Das sind die Schlüssel von Rom.

Nimm sie!

In Rom gibt es einen Platz.

Auf dem Platz gibt es eine Straße.

Auf der Straße gibt es ein Haus.

In dem Haus gibt es ein Bett.

Auf dem Bett gibt es eine Frau.

Bei den Füßen der Frau gibt es einen Papagei.

Und der Papagei sagt: Erzähl keine Lügen!

Die Frau ist nicht auf dem Bett.

Das Bette ist nicht in dem Haus.

Das Haus ist nicht auf der Straße.

Die Straße ist nicht auf dem Platz.

Der Platz ist nicht in Rom.

Und diese Schlüssel sind nicht die Schlüssel von Rom.

Verrückter Papagei!

Practice in German

This activity invites your children to re-tell the story of "The Keys to the Gates of Rome" using all of the new German words they have learned. This effectively tests their knowledge of the new words, and re-enforces the new words in their memory.

Instructions for This Page

Have your children look at the pictures and re-tell the story, using as much German as they can. Have them start with the picture of the keys and move around clockwise to the plaza and then the road and so on.

If your children are not ready to tell the story in German on their own, help them the first time through and have them try again, or have them go back and listen to the story a couple more times before trying to tell it again.

Audio Transcript

Narrator: Now see how much of this story you can tell. Look at the pictures in your activity book to remind you how the story goes. After your first telling, review the story before telling it again, even better. And after that, after further preparation, tell it again, better still.

Surprise Party

This section contains an audio transcript of the adventure story your children will hear on the tape.

Instructions for This Page

Have your children listen carefully as the adventure story is read on the tape. Encourage your children to take an active part in listening to the adventure story. Ask them to respond to things they hear and have them say out loud words said by the characters on the tape.

Younger children might enjoy coloring the picture as the adventure story is read. Older children may want to follow along with the written audio transcript provided in this *Parent's Guide*.

When your children get to the part of the adventure story where Nicole has prepared apple strudel, stop the tape and turn to the Recipes section at the back of this *Parent's Guide* to find the recipe. Try making some!

Audio Transcript

Narrator 2: The Adventure Continues: Surprise Party!

Max: That's cool to be able to tell that story by ourselves—and all it took was some practice!

Herr Einsiedler: Exactly, Max. And that is the piece of your treasure that I have for you: Practice. As you practice, things will become fixed in your mind. I even know a little song to help you remember this clue. In English it goes:

Yesterday, today, tomorrow practice.
Yesterday, today, tomorrow practice.
Yesterday, today, tomorrow practice.
Tomorrow will be better!

And in German it is:

Gestern, heute morgen üben.
Gestern, heute morgen üben.
Gestern, heute morgen üben.
Morgen wird es besser sein.

Serena: *Üben,* Practice. OK. Well, now that makes four clues: Build on what you know, Make learning fun, Don't stress, and Practice.

Herr Einsiedler: Very good. I'm glad you all are keeping track of the pieces of the treasure you've found so far. Now there is just one piece still to go, and you'll find that back in the village with Dieter.

Max: Yeah, I've wondered about that. The last X on the map is at the airport!

Herr Einsiedler: That's right, you'll get the last part of your treasure as you travel home. Now, my friends, you have just enough time to get back to

Continued from Children's Activity Book, page 105

the pier and catch the ferry back. Goodbye now! Auf Wiedersehen!

Serena: Auf Wiedersehen, Herr Einsiedler! Thanks for teaching us so much!

Max: *Ja, danke schön!*

Narrator: *"Danke schön,"* you say too as the three of you turn to go. You hurry down the lakeshore toward the ferry, and arrive in plenty of time to get a ride back to the main part of the valley.

You take your time getting back to Nicole and Dieter's house, and arrive just as it's beginning to get dark. To your surprise, you hear the sound of many voices inside the house! "I wonder who's here?" you say to Serena and Max.

Serena: Yeah. Nicole didn't say anything about having guests over tonight when we left this morning.

Max: Well, let's go in and find out who it is!

Narrator: As you open the door you, Serena and Max are greeted by a loud cheer: "Surprise!" everyone shouts.

Nicole: Welcome back! We thought we'd have a surprise party for you all since it's your last day here in the valley. Come in! I think you'll find that all of your friends are here.

Serena: Wow, Nicole, this is so nice of you.

Max: Yeah, everybody, thanks a lot for coming—*danke schön!*

Narrator: All of your friends from the valley are there, and you have a great time talking with them all. You're surprised to see how much German you have learned in just one week. Nicole has prepared a yummy apple strudel for dessert. Later, after all your friends have gone home at last, Nicole offers to tell you another story before you all go to sleep. "That sounds great, Nicole," you say.

Serena: Yeah, tell it to us.

Diglot Weave

This activity is a full-fledged diglot weave story, which means that unlike the diglot weave/rebus stories encountered so far, it uses no pictures to tell the story. The actual German words are used instead.

This story is taken directly from Power-Glide's adult German course, and is intended as a preparation for that course. In order to prepare your children to follow the plot of the story, many of the new words used in the story are taught through match and learn activities before the story begins.

Instructions for This Page

Have your children look at the picture in their activity book and listen to the introduction to the story of "The Broken Window."

Audio Transcript

Narrator 2: Activity: Diglot Weave Story. The Broken Window.

Narrator: As you all sit around the table, Nicole offers to tell you a story and teach you some more German at the same time. You eagerly agree and she begins her story, a story called "The Broken Window."

Match and Learn

This activity uses match and learn frames to introduce some new words that will be used in the story.

Instructions for This Page

Have your children look at the frames in their activity book and point to the pictures as the tape directs them. Have your children pause the tape as needed to have time to give their answers.

Audio Transcript

Narrator: Before I tell you Nicole's story, let me teach you a few new words so you can follow along. Look at the frames in your activity book and point to what you hear. Are you ready? OK, here we go!

Look at frame 1. Point to the *Wolf*, the wolf. It's in the top white box, right? Now point to the *Hund*. It's in the bottom gray box, right? Now point to the *Frau*. The *Frau* is in the bottom white box, right? Now point to the *Mann*, the man. He is in the top gray box. Did you point to them all? Good job.

Now look at frame 2. Point to the *Mädchen*. The girl is in the bottom gray box, right? Now point to the *Junge*. He is in the top white box, right? Now point to the group of three children. Can you guess what a group of children is called in German? They are called *Kinder*. Point to the *Kinder* in the top gray box. Now point to the last picture in this frame. What is it a picture of? A *Hund*? That's right!

Now look at frame 3. Point to the *Nase*. Did you remember that *Nase* is the word for nose? Good! Now point to the *Haus*. *Haus* is the German word for house. Now point to the *Fenster*. A *Fenster* is a window. Did you guess right? Good! Now point to the door. The German word for door is *Tür*. Say it out loud: *Tür*.

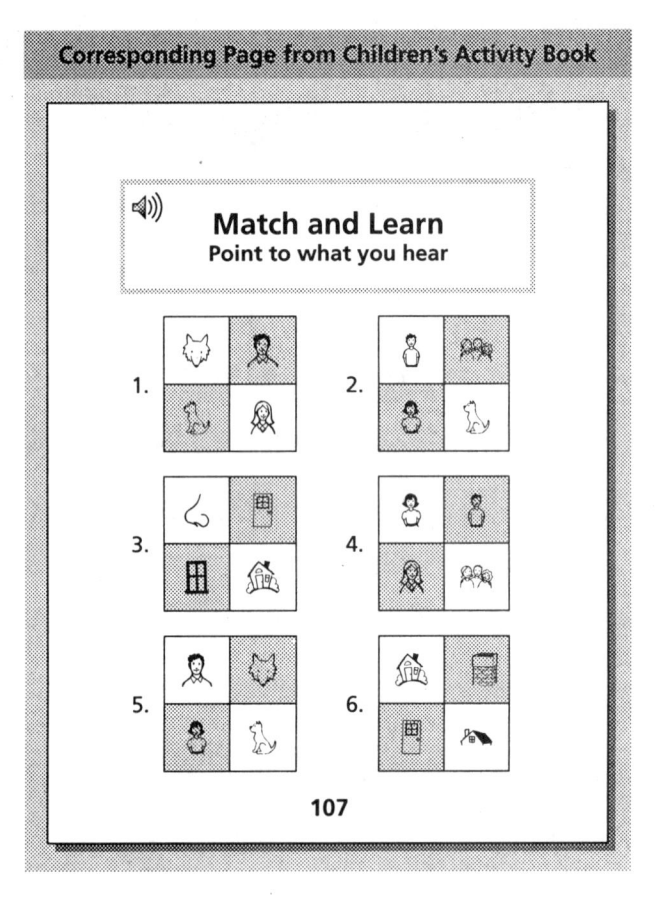

Now look at frame 4. Point to the *Junge*. Did you point to the boy? Good job. Now point to the *Kinder*. Did you point to the group of children? Well done. Now point to the *Frau*. You should have pointed to the woman. Now last of all, point to the *Mädchen*. Did you choose the girl? That's right.

Now look at frame 5. Point to the *Hund*. You should have pointed to the dog. Now point to the *Mädchen*. You should have pointed to the girl. Now point to the *Mann*. Did you point to the man? That's right! Now point to the *Wolf*. The *Wolf* is the wolf, right?

Now look at frame 6. Point to the *Haus*. The *Haus* is the house. Now point to the *Kamin*. Can you guess which one that is? Yes, it's the chimney. And what comes out of a *Kamin*? Why, *Rauch* of course! Smoke comes out of a *Kamin*! Now point to the *Tür*. Did you choose the door? Right on. Now last of all, point to the roof. Roof in German is *Dach*. Say it out loud: *Dach*. Well done.

Match and Learn

This activity uses match and learn frames to introduce some more new words that will be used in the story.

Instructions for This Page

Have your children look at the frames in their activity book and point to the pictures as the tape directs them.

Audio Transcript

Narrator: Here are just a few more new words you'll hear in the story. Look at the frames in your activity book and point to what you hear.

Look at frame 1. Point to the *Apfel*. Did you pick the apple? Right! Now point to the *Haus*. Did you choose the house? Good. Now point to the *Nase*. The *Nase* is the nose, of course! Now, last of all, point to the *Augen*. Did you point to the eyes? Right! *Augen* is the German word for eyes!

Now look at frame 2. Point to the *Kamin*. The *Kamin* is the chimney. Now point to the *Schwanz*. Did you choose the tail? In German the word for "tail" is *Schwanz*. Now point to the *Fenster*. Did you choose the window? Right on. Now point to the *Dach*. It's the roof, right?

Now look at frame 3. Point to the *Hund*. The *Hund* is the dog, right? Now point to the *Baum*. *Baum* is the German word for tree. Did you point to the tree? Good. Now point to the group of trees, the *Wald*. *Wald* is German for forest. Say it out loud: *Wald*. A *Wald* is made up of more than one *Baum*, right? Now, last of all, point to the *Tür*. The *Tür* is the door, right?

Now look at frame 4. Point to the *Wald*. Did you pick the forest? Good! Now point to the *Straße*.

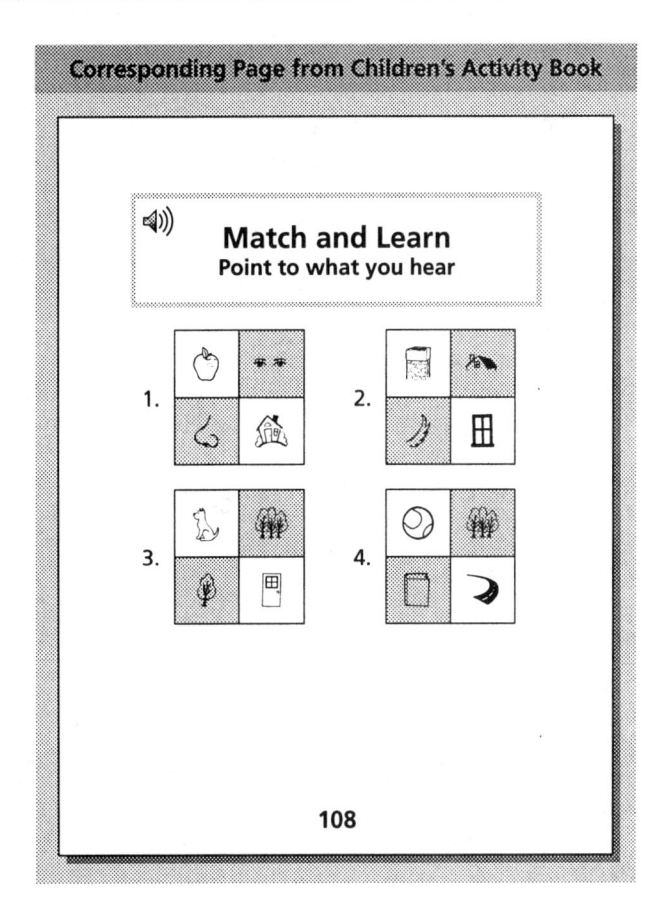

The *Straße* is the road. *Straße* means "road" in German. Now point to the book, the *Buch*. *Buch* is the German word for "book." Finally, point to the *Ball*. The *Ball* is in the top white box, right? Good memory!

Diglot Weave

The following is the complete diglot weave story of "The Broken Window," taken from the adult Power-Glide German course. As your children listen to the story, they will encounter the new German words they just learned, as well as other simple words and some words they have learned in previous activities.

The story format introduces the words in a fun and memorable way, and also lets your children see the actual German words on the page and begin to develop their reading ability.

Instructions for This Page

Have your children follow the words of the story in their activity book as they are read on the tape.

Audio Transcript

Narrator: Now listen as I tell the story, the *Geschichte*, "The Broken Window."

Would you like me to tell you *eine* short *Geschichte*? *Gut.* It is *eine Geschichte* about some naughty boys *und* girls.

(Now I'm not saying that you *ein ungezogener Junge bist. Aber* sometimes will *Jungen und Mädchen ungezogen* be.)

Corresponding Page from Children's Activity Book

Diglot Weave
The Broken Window

Would you like me to tell you *eine* short *Geschichte*? *Gut.* It is *eine Geschichte* about some naughty boys *und* girls.

(Now I'm not saying that you *ein ungezogener Junge bist. Aber* sometimes will *Jungen und Mädchen ungezogen* be.)

109

Diglot Weave

This is the next page of the diglot weave story of "The Broken Window."

Instructions for This Page

Have your children follow the words of the story in their activity book as they are read on the tape.

Audio Transcript

🔊 Narrator: *Die Jungen und Mädchen* in *dieser Geschichte* were playing *mit einem Ball* in *der* street...*ja, auf der Straße*...near *einem Haus*. Look at *das* picture...*das Bild. Hier ist das Haus und hier ist der Ball, der kleine Ball. Seht ihr* it *hier*? You can *sehen,* that *das Haus nicht ein* big *Haus ist...es ist nicht ein großes Haus, es ist* just *ein kleines Haus.*

Corresponding Page from Children's Activity Book

Die Jungen und Mädchen in *dieser Geschichte* were playing *mit einem Ball* in *der* street...*ja, auf der Straße*...near *einem Haus*. Look at *das* picture...*das Bild. Hier ist das Haus und hier ist der Ball, der kleine Ball. Seht ihr* it *hier*? You can *sehen,* that *das Haus nicht ein* big *Haus ist...es ist nicht ein großes Haus, es ist* just *ein kleines Haus.*

110

Diglot Weave

This is the next page of the diglot weave story of "The Broken Window."

Instructions for This Page

Have your children follow the words of the story in their activity book as they are read on the tape.

Audio Transcript

Narrator: Look *auf das Bild und* you can *sehen die* front *Tür von dem kleinen Haus.* Every *Haus,* whether it be *ein kleines Haus oder ein großes Haus,* has *eine Tür, nicht wahr?* Usually *ein Haus* has at least *zwei Türen, eine* front *Tür und eine* back *Tür.* Look...*schaut* again *auf das Bild und* you can *sehen* that on the second story *von dem kleinen Haus* there is *ein Fenster...ein Glasfenster auf der* left *Seite, und* another *Fenster auf der* right *Seite.*

Corresponding Page from Children's Activity Book

Look *auf das Bild und* you can *sehen die* front *Tür von dem kleinen Haus.* Every *Haus,* whether it be *ein kleines Haus oder ein großes Haus,* has *eine Tür, nicht wahr?* Usually *ein Haus* has at least *zwei Türen, eine* front *Tür und eine* back *Tür.* Look...*schaut* again *auf das Bild und* you can *sehen* that on the second story *von dem kleinen Haus* there is *ein Fenster... ein Glasfenster auf der* left *Seite, und* another *Fenster auf der* right *Seite.*

111

Diglot Weave

This is the next page of the diglot weave story of "The Broken Window."

Instructions for This Page

Have your children follow the words of the story in their activity book as they are read on the tape.

Audio Transcript

Narrator: *Schaut* again *auf das kleine Haus* in *diesem Bild*. Of course, on top *von dem Haus* there is *ein Dach*. On top *von* every *Haus* there's *ein Dach, nicht wahr?* Notice that sticking up out *von dem Dach ist ein* brick *Kamin*. *Und* billowing out of *dem Kamin ist Rauch*. That is what *ein Kamin* is for, to let *Rauch* out *von dem Haus, nicht wahr?*

Corresponding Page from Children's Activity Book

Schaut again *auf das kleine Haus* in *diesem Bild*. Of course, on top *von dem Haus* there is *ein Dach*. On top *von* every *Haus* there's *ein Dach, nicht wahr?* Notice that sticking up out *von dem Dach ist ein* brick *Kamin*. *Und* billowing out of *dem Kamin ist Rauch*. That is what *ein Kamin* is for, to let *Rauch* out *von dem Haus, nicht wahr?*

112

Diglot Weave

This is the next page of the diglot weave story of "The Broken Window."

Instructions for This Page

Have your children follow the words of the story in their activity book as they are read on the tape.

Audio Transcript

Narrator: Now I'll continue *meine Geschichte*, talking about what *ist* in *dem Bild. Schaut auf der* right *Seite von dem Bild. Auf dieser Seite von dem Bild* can you *sehen* many Christmas trees, many *Tannenbäume*? There is a famous German Christmas carol—*Oh Tannenbaum, oh Tannenbaum.* You know it, *nicht wahr?* Those *Bäume* there *auf der rechten Seite* represent a *Wald*—not a bank vault, but a forest or wildwood—a somewhat dangerous place.

Corresponding Page from Children's Activity Book

Now I'll continue *meine Geschichte*, talking about what *ist* in *dem Bild. Schaut auf der* right *Seite von dem Bild. Auf dieser Seite von dem Bild* can you *sehen* many Christmas trees, many *Tannenbäume*? There is a famous German Christmas carol—*Oh Tannenbaum, oh Tannenbaum.* You know it, *nicht wahr?* Those *Bäume* there *auf der rechten Seite* represent a *Wald*—not a bank vault, but a forest or wildwood—a somewhat dangerous place.

113

Diglot Weave

This is the next page of the diglot weave story of "The Broken Window."

Instructions for This Page

Have your children follow the words of the story in their activity book as they are read on the tape.

Audio Transcript

Narrator: *Wenn* you *schauen* closely at *den Wald* you will see something sticking out from *unter einem Baum. Und* if you look *sehr* close, you'll see *einen* small arrow... *einen kleinen Pfeil,* pointing it out. *Seht ihr den kleinen Pfeil? Hier ist er.* Now what could *der kleine Pfeil* be pointing to? *Einen Schwanz,* perhaps. Could it be the tail *(der Schwanz) eines Wolfes?* Do you think *der kleine Pfeil* points to *den Schwanz eines Wolfes?* I told you there is danger in *dem Wald.* There could be *ein Wolf* in *dem Wald, oder ein Bär!*

Corresponding Page from Children's Activity Book

Wenn you *schauen* closely at *den Wald* you will see something sticking out from *unter einem Baum. Und* if you look *sehr* close, you'll see *einen* small arrow... *einen kleinen Pfeil,* pointing it out. *Seht ihr den kleinen Pfeil? Hier ist er.* Now what could *der kleine Pfeil* be pointing to? *Einen Schwanz,* perhaps. Could it be the tail *(der Schwanz) eines Wolfes?* Do you think *der kleine Pfeil* points to *den Schwanz eines Wolfes?* I told you there is danger in *dem Wald.* There could be *ein Wolf* in *dem Wald, oder ein Bär!*

114

Diglot Weave

This is the next page of the diglot weave story of "The Broken Window."

Instructions for This Page

Have your children follow the words of the story in their activity book as they are read on the tape.

Audio Transcript

Narrator: I have told you that in *dieser Geschichte* there are boys and girls...*Jungen und Mädchen*; actually, there are *zwei Jungen und zwei Mädchen*. *Aber* there are other *Personen* in *der Geschichte* as well. Now I'll introduce them. Besides *die zwei Jungen und die zwei Mädchen* there's *ein Mann und eine Oma*. *Ihr* can *nicht* see her in *dem Bild, aber die Oma* is coming down the *Straße*. As for the *Mann, er ist* in *dem Haus*. *Er* is sitting at *dem Fenster*. Oh, but you suspect there might be another character, do you? Perhaps...a big, bad *Wolf* hiding *unter dem Baum in dem Wald!* You're afraid *daß der Wolf* could hurt *die ungezogenen Jungen und Mädchen*. Well just listen as *meine Geschichte* unfolds *und* you'll find out what happens, *was passiert*.

Corresponding Page from Children's Activity Book

I have told you that in *dieser Geschichte* there are boys and girls...*Jungen und Mädchen*; actually, there are *zwei Jungen und zwei Mädchen. Aber* there are other *Personen* in *der Geschichte* as well. Now I'll introduce them. Besides *die zwei Jungen und die zwei Mädchen* there's *ein Mann und eine Oma. Ihr* can *nicht* see her in *dem Bild, aber die Oma* is coming down the *Straße*. As for the *Mann, er ist* in *dem Haus. Er* is sitting at *dem Fenster*. Oh, but you suspect there might be another character, do you? Perhaps...a big, bad *Wolf* hiding *unter dem Baum in dem Wald!* You're afraid *daß der Wolf* could hurt *die ungezogenen Jungen und Mädchen*. Well just listen as *meine Geschichte* unfolds *und* you'll find out what happens, *was passiert*.

Diglot Weave

This is the next page of the diglot weave story of "The Broken Window."

Instructions for This Page

Have your children follow the words of the story in their activity book as they are read on the tape.

Audio Transcript

Narrator: At this very moment, *die Oma* was coming down *die Straße,* walking toward *dem Haus. Diese Jungen und Mädchen* were playing with *einem Ball auf der Straße* when one *von* the *Jungen* threw *den Ball, und der Ball* flew up toward *dem Haus.* Try to guess: will *der Ball* crash through *die Tür? Nein, der Ball* won't crash through *die Tür.* Will *der Ball* go down *den Kamin? Nein, der Ball* won't go down *den Kamin.* Santa Claus may go down *den Kamin,* but *nicht dieser Ball.* Will *der Ball* hit *das Fenster? Ja!* As you might guess, *der Ball* goes crash! right into *das Fenster* where *der Mann sitzt.*

Corresponding Page from Children's Activity Book

At this very moment, *die Oma* was coming down *die Straße,* walking toward *dem Haus. Diese Jungen und Mädchen* were playing with *einem Ball auf der Straße* when one *von* the *Jungen* threw *den Ball, und der Ball* flew up toward *dem Haus.* Try to guess: will *der Ball* crash through *die Tür? Nein, der Ball* won't crash through *die Tür.* Will *der Ball* go down *den Kamin? Nein, der Ball* won't go down *den Kamin.* Santa Claus may go down *den Kamin,* but *nicht dieser Ball.* Will *der Ball* hit *das Fenster? Ja!* As you might guess, *der Ball* goes crash! right into *das Fenster* where *der Mann sitzt.*

116

Diglot Weave

This is the next page of the diglot weave story of "The Broken Window."

Instructions for This Page

Have your children follow the words of the story in their activity book as they are read on the tape.

Audio Transcript

🔊 Narrator: In fact *der Ball* smacks *den* poor *Mann* right *auf die Nase*. Oh, no! *Ist der Mann zornig?* Oh *ja, er ist sehr zornig*.

Now, do you think *daß der zornige Mann* climbs up on *das Dach und* jumps onto *den Baum? Nein. Denkt ihr, daß die Jungen und Mädchen* go *und* knock on *die Tür? Nein. Denkt ihr, daß die Jungen und Mädchen* run to *dem Apfelbaum und* steal *den großen* juicy *Apfel? Nein.*

Corresponding Page from Children's Activity Book

In fact *der Ball* smacks *den* poor *Mann* right *auf die Nase*. Oh, no! *Ist der Mann zornig?* Oh *ja, er ist sehr zornig*.

Now, do you think *daß der zornige Mann* climbs up on *das Dach und* jumps onto *den Baum? Nein. Denkt ihr, daß die Jungen und Mädchen* go *und* knock on *die Tür? Nein. Denkt ihr, daß die Jungen und Mädchen* run to *dem Apfelbaum und* steal *den großen* juicy *Apfel? Nein.*

Diglot Weave

This is the next page of the diglot weave story of "The Broken Window."

Instructions for This Page

Have your children follow the words of the story in their activity book as they are read on the tape.

Audio Transcript

Narrator: *Was* happened after that? *Dies ist* what actually *passiert: Der Mann ist* angry...*zornig, sehr zornig und* calls out: *"Jungen! Mädchen! Halt, Halt!" Aber die ungezogenen Kinder* don't pay attention. *Sie* run up *die Straße.* Why do they run up the street? You know, *daß der Mann sehr zornig ist.* Wouldn't your daddy be *zornig wenn* some *Junge oder Mädchen* came along *und* threw *einen Ball* right through his *Fenster? Und* especially *wenn der Ball* smacked him right *auf die Nase?*

Corresponding Page from Children's Activity Book

Was happened after that? *Dies ist* what actually *passiert: Der Mann ist* angry...*zornig, sehr zornig und* calls out: *"Jungen! Mädchen! Halt, Halt!" Aber die ungezogenen Kinder* don't pay attention. *Sie* run up *die Straße.* Why do they run up the street? You know, *daß der Mann sehr zornig ist.* Wouldn't your daddy be *zornig wenn* some *Junge oder Mädchen* came along *und* threw *einen Ball* right through his *Fenster? Und* especially *wenn der Ball* smacked him right *auf die Nase?*

118

Diglot Weave

This is the next page of the diglot weave story of "The Broken Window."

Instructions for This Page

Have your children follow the words of the story in their activity book as they are read on the tape.

Audio Transcript

Narrator: Did anyone else see *den Ball* smash *das Fenster und* smack *den Mann* right *auf die Nase? Ja! Die Oma sah* was *passiert ist. Die Kinder* start to run up *die Straße. Aber* then *sie* look up *und sehen die Oma* walking down *die Straße* toward them. *Die Kinder* know *daß die Oma alles sah* was *passiert ist. Die Oma* sees *die Jungen und Mädchen* running up *die Straße und sie* calls out: *"Jungen! Mädchen! Halt!" Aber die ungezogenen Kinder* pay no attention. Instead, they run *zu dem Wald. Sie* fear *den Mann und die Oma* mehr than *den Wolf!*

Corresponding Page from Children's Activity Book

Did anyone else see *den Ball* smash *das Fenster und* smack *den Mann* right *auf die Nase? Ja! Die Oma sah* was *passiert ist. Die Kinder* start to run up *die Straße. Aber* then *sie* look up *und sehen die Oma* walking down *die Straße* toward them. *Die Kinder* know *daß die Oma alles sah* was *passiert ist. Die Oma* sees *die Jungen und Mädchen* running up *die Straße und sie* calls out: *"Jungen! Mädchen! Halt!" Aber die ungezogenen Kinder* pay no attention. Instead, they run *zu dem Wald. Sie* fear *den Mann und die Oma* mehr than *den Wolf!*

Diglot Weave

This is the next page of the diglot weave story of "The Broken Window."

Instructions for This Page

Have your children follow the words of the story in their activity book as they are read on the tape.

Audio Transcript

Narrator: Just as they enter *den Wald, sehen die kleinen Jungen und Mädchen* something hiding behind *einem Baum*. Could it be *der* Big Bad *Wolf*? *Oder* is it only Rover, *der große* old *Hund, der* loves to play in *dem Wald mit Jungen und Mädchen? Nein, es ist nicht Rover. Es ist der Wolf! Und er* plans to hurt *diese kleinen Jungen und Mädchen*.

Corresponding Page from Children's Activity Book

Just as they enter *den Wald, sehen die kleinen Jungen und Mädchen* something hiding behind *einem Baum*. Could it be *der* Big Bad *Wolf*? *Oder* is it only Rover, *der große* old *Hund, der* loves to play in *dem Wald mit Jungen und Mädchen? Nein, es ist nicht Rover. Es ist der Wolf! Und er* plans to hurt *diese kleinen Jungen und Mädchen*.

120

Diglot Weave

This is the next page of the diglot weave story of "The Broken Window."

Instructions for This Page

Have your children follow the words of the story in their activity book as they are read on the tape.

Audio Transcript

Narrator: Just as *der Wolf* charges, *sehen die kleinen Jungen und Mädchen den großen* old *Hund* that loves to run and play in *dem Wald mit Jungen und Mädchen.* "Rover! Rover!" *schreien sie.* Rover *kommt und* chases off *den Wolf und* saves *die Kinder.* Rover *ist ein* hero—*ein Held!*

Corresponding Page from Children's Activity Book

Just as *der Wolf* charges, *sehen die kleinen Jungen und Mädchen den großen* old *Hund* that loves to run and play in *dem Wald mit Jungen und Mädchen.* "Rover! Rover!" *schreien sie.* Rover *kommt und* chases off *den Wolf und* saves *die Kinder.* Rover *ist ein* hero—*ein Held!*

Diglot Weave

This is the last page of the diglot weave story of "The Broken Window."

Instructions for This Page

Have your children follow the words of the story in their activity book as they are read on the tape.

Audio Transcript

Narrator: *Die Kinder* run out *von dem Wald. Sie* go back to *dem Haus,* knock on *die Tür und* offer to pay *für das zerbrochene Fenster.* Now *ist der Mann nicht* anymore zornig. *Er* says: *"Ach, meine lieben Jungen und Mädchen. Ich bin sooo* relieved, sooo glad, *daß der Wolf* did not hurt you."

Corresponding Page from Children's Activity Book

Die Kinder run out *von dem Wald. Sie* go back to *dem Haus,* knock on *die Tür und* offer to pay *für das zerbrochene Fenster.* Now *ist der Mann nicht* anymore zornig. *Er* says: *"Ach, meine lieben Jungen und Mädchen. Ich bin sooo* relieved, sooo glad, *daß der Wolf* did not hurt you."

Flying Home

This section contains an audio transcript of the adventure story your children will hear on the tape.

Instructions for This Page

Have your children listen carefully as the adventure story is read on the tape.

Encourage your children to take an active part in listening to the adventure story. Ask them to respond to things they hear and have them say out loud words said by the characters on the tape. Younger children might enjoy coloring the picture as the adventure story is read. Older children may want to follow along with the written audio transcript provided in this *Parent's Guide*.

Audio Transcript

Narrator 2: The Adventure Continues: Flying Home

Max: Thanks for telling us that story, Nicole. I think I'm learning more German from all the stories people are telling us than from anything else. It's a really cool way to learn new words and stuff.

Nicole: Yes, it is fun, isn't it? And now, you all need some sleep. You'll have a big day tomorrow!

Narrator: You, Serena and Max sleep very comfortably in the loft again, and in the morning Dieter wakes you early and you stumble down the ladder, still tired but excited now to be on your way home.

Dieter: *Guten Morgen,* my friends! Well, this is it, the day you all fly home! Are you ready?

Max: Yeah, I think we are. It has been lots of fun visiting your valley, though! I hope to come again to visit soon.

Nicole: That would be wonderful—*Wunderbar!* Well, I guess this is time to say goodbye. *Auf Wiedersehen,* my friends!

Serena: *Auf Wiedersehen,* Nicole. *Danke schön* for being so nice to us.

Narrator: *"Ja,"* you add, "maybe Serena and I can write you letters in German once we're home."

Nicole: I would like that very much. Goodbye!

Narrator: You, Serena and Max walk with Dieter into the village. You get there just as the sun is coming up over the tall hills that surround the valley. Dieter leads you through the village to a small airport on the other side. Soon after you get there you hear the hum of a distant engine, and an airplane flies over the horizon and begins to drop slowly down toward the airport. It touches down on the runway and taxis over to where you and a few other people are standing.

Continued from Children's Activity Book, page 123

Max: Well, Dieter, I guess this is where you say Auf Wiedersehen, too, right?

Dieter: Actually, Max, no. I'm flying with you this morning. I have some business to do in a city near where Max's parents live, and this seems a good time to do it. Besides, flying with you will give me a few more minutes to talk with you all. Come on, let's get aboard the plane.

Narrator: So you, Serena, Max and Dieter climb aboard the airplane and after just a few minutes it takes off once more, circling higher and higher until it can finally get up out of the valley. As the plane drones along, Dieter talks with you.

Dieter: You three have been great adventurers these last few days. My friends have all been impressed by how quickly you've learned so much German. I wonder now, just how much you have learned. I challenge you to show me!

Dieter's Challenge

This section reviews and reinforces much of the course material, using a variety of activity types.

This first activity begins reviewing some of the vocabulary learned in this course. It uses the familiar match and learn frames.

Instructions for This Page

Have your children point to the pictures in the various frames as directed by the tape.

Since this activity asks your children to remember words which they may not have seen for some time, it is especially important to encourage them to guess boldly and not worry if they do not remember every word perfectly. Also, you may wish to go back to particular sections and review if your children seem to have a hard time recalling particular words.

Frame 5 departs a little from the activity it's based on, "A Girl and a Rat." Rather than having the girl interacting with a rat, we used the word for mouse that your children learned from "A Farmer and a Turnip."

Audio Transcript

Narrator 2: Activity: Dieter's Challenge!

Narrator: For the first part of his language challenge, Dieter says German words you have learned and asks you to point to pictures of what he says. Are you ready for the challenge? All right, here we go! Point to what you hear.

First, look at frame 1 in your activity book. Point to the *Suppe*. Did you point to the soup? Good! Now point to the *Schuh*. It's the shoe, right? Now point to the *Ball*. A *Ball* is a ball, right? Now, last of all, point to the *Stein*. The *Stein* is the rock, right?

Now look at frame 2. Point to the box with *einem Quadrat, einem Kreis, und zwei Dreiecke*. It's the bottom white box, right? Now point to the box with *einem Kreis, zwei Quadrate, und einer Linie*. It's the top gray box, isn't it? Now point to the box with *zwei Kreise und zwei Linien*. It's the bottom gray box, right? Now, what's in the last box? *Ein Quadrat und ein Kreis,* right? That's right!

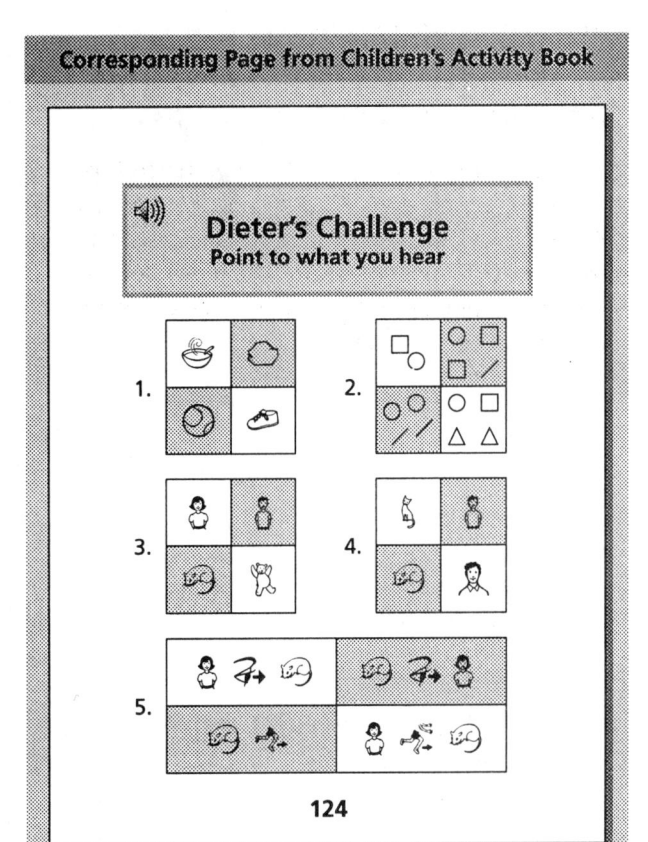

Now look at frame 3. Point to the *Mädchen*. It's the girl, right? Now point to the *Jungen*. That is the boy, right? Now point to the *Maus*. It's the mouse, right? And what's the last picture? That's right—it is a *Bär*, a bear.

Now look at frame 4. Point to the *Mann*. It's the man, right? Good. Now point to the *Junge*. It's the boy, right? Good. Now point to the *Katze*. That's the cat, right? And finally, point to the *Maus*. It's the mouse, right? Well done.

Now look at frame 5. Point to *Maus läuft*. It's the bottom gray box, right? Now point to *Maus sieht Mädchen*. It is the top gray box, right? Now point to *Mädchen jagt Maus*. It's the bottom white box, right? Good.

Power-Glide **Children's German**

Match and Learn

This activity continues reviewing some of the vocabulary learned in this course.

Instructions for This Page

Have your children point to the pictures in the various frames as directed by the tape.

Audio Transcript

Narrator: Here are some more frames. See how many of these words you can remember.

Look at frame 6. Point to the *Sonne*. It is in the top white box, right? Yes. Now point to the *Bauer*. It is in the bottom white box? Yes, it is. Now point to the *Frau*. The *Frau* is in the bottom gray box, right? Yes.

Now look at frame 7. Point to the thing that is *rot*. Did you point to the cherries? That's right! Cherries are *rot*—red! Now point to the thing that is *gelb* color. Did you point to the banana? Well done! The banana is yellow, *gelb*. Now point to the thing that is *blau*. Did you choose the water? Water is *blau* in the ocean.

Now look at frame 8. Point to the thing that is *lila*. Did you point to the grapes? That's right! Grapes are *lila*—they are purple! Now point to the thing that is *orange*. Did you point to the carrot? Carrots are orange aren't they? Now point to the thing that is *rosa*. Did you choose the flower? Good! The flower is *rosa*—pink!

Now look at frame 9. Point to the *Straße*. Did you point to the street? Good! Now point to the *Platz*. Did you point to the plaza? That's right. And now, point to the *Papagei*. That's the parrot, right? Finally, point to the *Schlüssel*. It's the keys, right?

Corresponding Page from Children's Activity Book

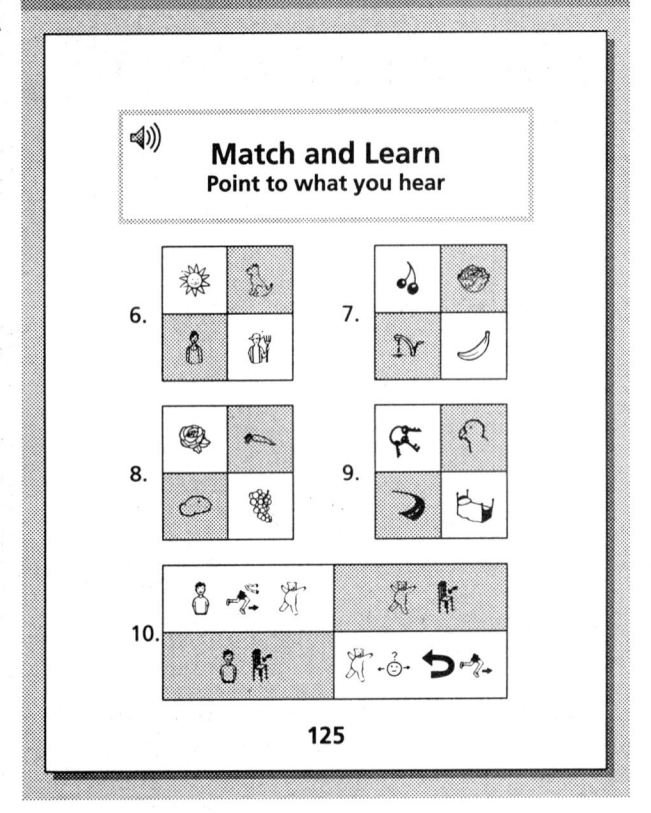

Match and Learn
Point to what you hear

Now look at frame 10. Point to *der Junge setzt sich*. Did you point to the bottom gray box? Good. Now point to *Bär setzt sich*. It's is in the top gray box, right? Point to *der Bär zögert, dreht sich um, läuft*. This is in the bottom white box, right? Now point to *der Junge jagt den Bär*. Did you point to the top white box? Good.

Dieter's Challenge

Match and Learn

This activity continues reviewing vocabulary.

Instructions for This Page

Have your children point to the pictures in the various frames as directed by the tape.

Audio Transcript

Narrator: Here are some more frames. See how many of these words you can remember.

Look at frame 11. Point to the *Hand*. Did you point to the hand? Good! Now point to the *Kopf*. Did you point to the head? Good! Finally, point to the *Bein*. Did you point to the leg? That's right.

Now look at frame 12. Point to the *Bein*. It's in the top white box, right? Now point to the *Fuß*. That's the foot, right? Now point to the *Mund*. It's the mouth, right? Finally, point to the *Haar*. It's in the bottom gray box, right? Good.

Now look at frame 13. Point to the *Kinn*. Did you point to the chin? Good! Now point to the *Auge*. Did you point to the eye? Good! Finally, point to the *Ohr*. Did you point to the ear? That's right!

Now look at frame 14. Point to the *Haus*. The *Haus* is the house, right? Yes. Now point to the *Kamin*. Can you guess which one that is? Yes, it's the chimney. And what comes out of a *Kamin*? Point to what comes out of a *Kamin* and say what it is out loud. Did you point to the *Rauch* and say *Rauch* out loud? Good!

Now look at frame 15. Point to the *Ball*. It's the ball, isn't it? Now point to the *Nase*. Did you choose the nose? Fantastic! Now point to the *Apfel*. It's the apple, right?

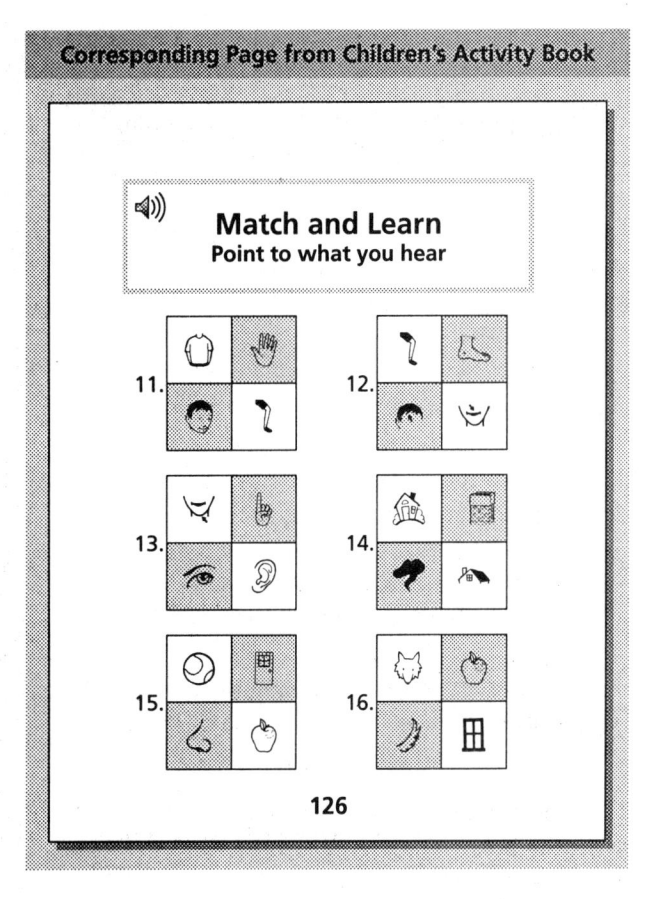

Now look at frame 16. Point to the *Apfel*. That's the top gray box, right? Now point to the *Wolf*. That's the wolf. Now point to the *Schwanz*. Did you point to the tail? Super! Now point to the *Fenster*. That's the window, right? Good.

Match and Learn

This activity tests your children's memory of the vocabulary just reviewed. In this activity words from the entire course are mixed together.

Instructions for This Page

Have your children point to the pictures as directed by the tape. Have your children pause the tape as needed to give their answers.

💡 This activity is more challenging than the previous ones. Encourage your children to do their best and not worry if they don't remember all the words perfectly.

Audio Transcript

Narrator: You did a good job with those matching frames! Once Dieter has challenged your ability to remember words of the same kind grouped together, he mixes all the words up and challenges you to remember them that way. Let's see if you can! In this activity, I'll simply say the German word, followed by the English one.

Look at the frame on your activity book page. Point to the *Kreis*. The circle. Now the *Arm*. The arm. The *Stein*. The rock. The *Haus*. The house. The *Mädchen*. The girl. The *Wolf*. The wolf. The *Frau*. The woman. The *Ohr*. The ear. The *Rauch*. The smoke.

How did you do? Did you remember most of them? Good!

Corresponding Page from Children's Activity Book

Match and Learn
Point to what you hear

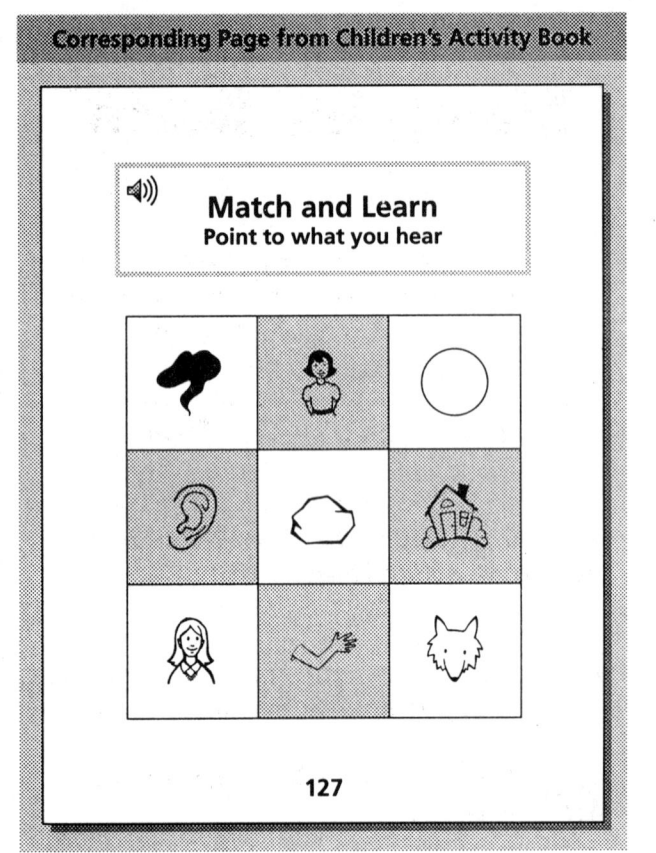

Match and Learn

This activity tests your children's memory of the vocabulary just reviewed. In this activity words from the entire course are mixed together.

Instructions for This Page

Have your children point to the pictures as directed by the tape. Have your children pause the tape as needed to have time to give their answers.

Audio Transcript

Narrator: Here is another frame. Point to what you hear.

A *Junge*. A boy. A *Baum*. A tree. Something that is *rot*. The cherries. A *Fuß*. A foot. A *Dach*. A roof. A *Dreieck*. A triangle. A *Maus*. A mouse. A *Nase*. A nose. A *Linie*. A line.

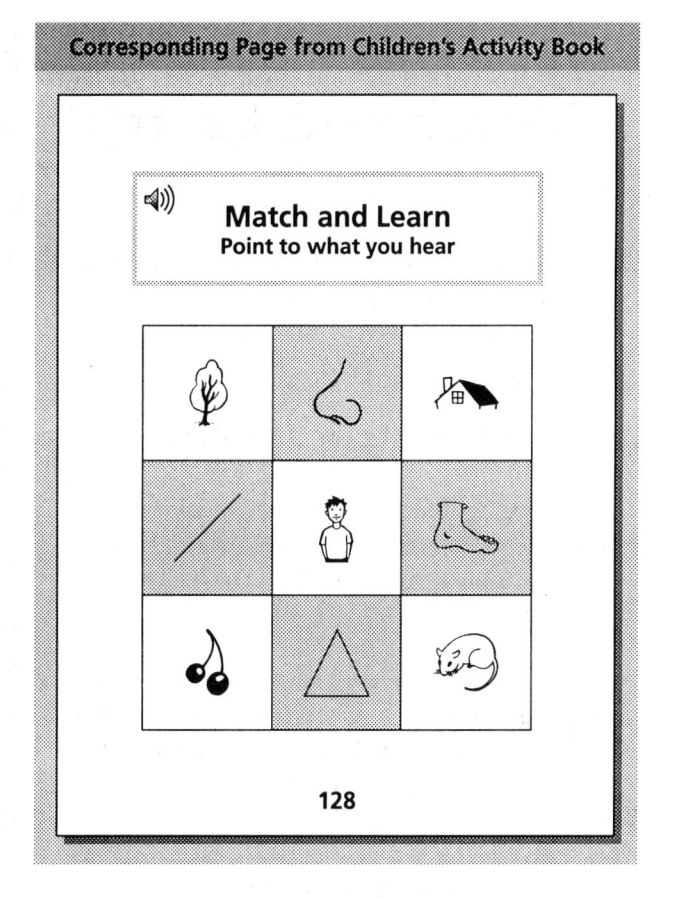

Match and Learn

This activity tests your children's memory of the vocabulary just reviewed. In this activity words from the entire course are mixed together.

Instructions for This Page

Have your children point to the pictures as directed by the tape. Have your children pause the tape as needed to have time to give their answers.

Audio Transcript

Narrator: Here is one last frame. Point to what you hear.

A *Quadrat*. A square. An *Auge*. An eye. A *Bär*. A bear. Something that is *gelb*. The banana. A *Hund*. A dog. A *Stein*. A rock. A *Ball*. A ball. A *Hand*. A hand. A *Kopf*. A head.

Corresponding Page from Children's Activity Book

Match and Learn
Point to what you hear

Diglot Weave

This activity is a rebus story with German words in small print where pictures should be. Your children's task is to put in pictures in the right places.

Instructions for This Page

Have your children find and cut out the page of picture stickers at the back of their activity book. Have them look over the pictures before the story begins, so they know what their choices are. As the story is told on the tape, have them put the stickers over the small-print German words found in circles throughout the story.

💡 Have your children pause the tape as needed to have time to find and put in the right stickers.

Audio Transcript

🔊 Narrator: After you answer Dieter's questions, he offers to tell you part of the story of "A Hungry Giant" again, using mostly German words. Your challenge is to put in pictures for the German words he uses. Look at the story in your activity book. Do you see all the circles with small German words written inside them? That is where the pictures go. Take out the stickers included with your course. Look through the them all, then start listening to the story.

Do you have the stickers? Have you looked at all of the pictures? Good! Dieter began:

One morning before breakfast *mein Vater* took a walk and saw *eine Fliege* that was caught in a spider's web. He watched *die Spinne* come and eat the fly.

Corresponding Page from Children's Activity Book

🔊 **Diglot Weave**
A Hungry Giant

One morning before breakfast *mein Vater* took a walk and saw *eine* (fliege) that was caught in a spider's web. He watched *die* (spinne) come and eat the fly. *Gut!* ("Good!") thought *mein Vater*. "*Die* (spinne) has eaten *die* (fliege). I don't like flies... *Ich mag keine Fliegen.*"

130

Gut! ("Good!") thought *mein Vater*. "*Die Spinne* has eaten *die Fliege*. I don't like flies... *Ich mag keine Fliegen.*"

Diglot Weave

This page continues Dieter's story.

Instructions for This Page

As the story is told on the tape, have your children put the stickers over the small-print German words found in circles throughout the story. Have your children pause the tape as needed to have time to find and put in the right stickers.

Audio Transcript

🔊 Narrator: A moment later, a *Vogel* came and *fraß die Spinne*. "*Gut,*" thought *mein Vater*. "*Der Vogel* has eaten *die Spinne. Ich mag keine Spinnen.*"

The next moment *eine Katze* came along *und fraß den Vogel. Und mein Vater dachte*: "Too bad; *Ich mag Vögel.*"

Corresponding Page from Children's Activity Book

A moment later, a (vogel) came and (fraß) die (spinne). "Gut," thought mein Vater. "Der Vogel has eaten die Spinne. Ich mag keine Spinnen." The next moment eine (katze) came along und fraß den (vogel). Und mein Vater (dachte): "Too bad; Ich mag (vogel)."

131

Diglot Weave

This page continues Dieter's story.

Instructions for This Page

As the story is told on the tape, have your children put the stickers over the small-print German words found in circles throughout the story. Have your children pause the tape as needed to have time to find and put in the right stickers.

Audio Transcript

Narrator: The next moment *eine Schlange* came along *und fraß die Katze. Und mein Vater dachte:* "Too bad, *ich mag Katzen.*"

The next moment *ein Schwein* came along *und fraß die Schlange. Und mein Vater dachte:* "Gut, *das Schwein* has eaten *die Schlange. Ich mag keine Schlangen.*"

Corresponding Page from Children's Activity Book

The next moment *eine* (schlange) came along *und* (fraß) *die Katze. Und mein Vater dachte:* "Too bad, *ich mag* (katzen)." The next moment *ein* (schwein) came along *und fraß die* (schlange). *Und mein Vater* (dachte): "Gut, *das Schwein* has eaten *die Schlange. Ich mag keine Schlangen.*"

132

Diglot Weave

This page continues Dieter's story.

Instructions for This Page

As the story is told on the tape, have your children put the stickers over the small-print German words found in circles throughout the story. Have your children pause the tape as needed to have time to find and put in the right stickers.

Audio Transcript

Narrator: Before long *ein Leopard* came along *und fraß das Schwein. Und mein Vater dachte:* "*Gut, ein Leopard* has eaten *das Schwein.* This is exiting!"

A while later *ein Krokodil* came along *und fraß den Leopard. Und mein Vater dachte:* "Wow, *ein Krokodil* has eaten *den Leopard.* This is really exciting. What will happen now?"

Corresponding Page from Children's Activity Book

Before long *ein* (leopard) came along *und fraß das* (schwein). *Und mein Vater dachte:* "*Gut, ein Leopard* has eaten *das Schwein.* This is exiting!" A while later *ein* (krokodil) came along *und* (fraß) *den Leopard. Und mein Vater* (dachte): "Wow, *ein* (krokodil) has eaten *den Leopard.* This is really exciting. What will happen now?"

133

Dieter's Challenge

Diglot Weave

This page continues Dieter's story.

Instructions for This Page

As the story is told on the tape, have your children put the stickers over the small-print German words found in circles throughout the story. Have your children pause the tape as needed to have time to find and put in the right stickers.

Audio Transcript

Narrator: Before long *ein Nilpferd* came along *und fraß das Krokodil. Und mein Vater dachte:* "Wow, *ein Nilpferd* has eaten *das Krokodil.* What will happen now?"

A moment later *ein Wal* came along *und fraß das Nilpferd. Und mein Vater dachte:* "Wow, this is too much."

Corresponding Page from Children's Activity Book

Before long *ein Nilpferd* came along *und fraß das* (krokodil). *Und mein Vater dachte:* "Wow, *ein* (nilpferd) has eaten *das Krokodil.* What will happen now?" A moment later *ein* (wal) came along *und* (fraß) *das* (nilpferd). *Und mein Vater dachte:* "Wow, this is too much."

134

Diglot Weave

This page concludes Dieter's story.

Instructions for This Page

As the story is told on the tape, have your children put the stickers over the small-print German words found in circles throughout the story. Have your children pause the tape as needed to have time to find and put in the right stickers.

Audio Transcript

Narrator: Just then *eine Hand* reached down from the sky and picked up the whale. *Mein Vater* looked up just as *der Riese* swallowed the whole whale. And he thought: "Wow, this is the first time I've seen a giant.

Maybe he's still *hungrig*. I'd better get out of here!" And he ran home as fast as he could.

Corresponding Page from Children's Activity Book

Just then *eine* (hand) reached down from the sky and picked up the whale. *Mein Vater* looked up just as *der* (riese) swallowed the whole whale. And he thought: "Wow, this is the first time I've seen a giant. Maybe he's still *hungrig*. I'd better get out of here!" And he ran home as fast as he could.

135

Draw and Learn

This activity invites your children to draw a picture following instructions in German.

Instructions for This Page

Have your children listen to the instructions given on the tape and draw what they hear. Although general instructions are given on where to draw each object, there is no "right" way to draw the picture (so long as the right objects are drawn), and no picture key is provided. Once your children have drawn the picture, have them color it and encourage them to show it and other drawings they make to friends, and tell them what the things in the picture are in German!

💡 Have your children pause the tape as needed to draw.

Audio Transcript

🔊 Narrator: Once you have finished those activities, Dieter gives you some new challenges. On this chalkboard I'll tell you what to draw, and you draw it, OK? Here we go!

First, near the bottom of your chalkboard in the middle, draw a *Haus*. Are you finished? Good.

Now, draw a *Straße* leading up to the *Haus*.

Next, draw a *Baum* next to the *Haus*.

And on one side of the *Haus,* draw a *Mädchen* with a *Katze* by her side.

And on the other side of the *Haus*, draw a *Maus*, hiding from the *Katze*.

Were you able to draw all that? Good work!

Now that it's drawn, it's time to color it.

Corresponding Page from Children's Activity Book

🔊 **Draw and Learn**
Draw what you hear

136

First, color the sky *blau*

Next, color the *Straße schwarz*.

Next, color the trunk of the *Baum braun*, and the top of the *Baum grün*.

Next, color the walls of the *Haus orange*, and the *Dach rot*.

Next, color the *Katze gelb* and the *Maus weiß*.

And last of all, color the *Mädchen's* dress or pants *rosa* or *lila*, whichever you prefer.

Are you finished? Good! Now you can also show your picture to other people and tell them what the parts and the colors are in German!

Story Telling

This activity provides pictures and a plot chain, and invites your children to use the pictures to make up stories of their own.

Instructions for This Page

Have your children remove the Pictograph Cut-out page from the back of their activity books and cut out the pictures along the light gray lines. Once they are all cut up, have them arrange the pictures in order along the blank plot chain on this page in order to create a story. Once the pictures are arranged in order, have your children tell you the story the pictures represent. Then see if they can rearrange the pictures to make another story, and another.

Audio Transcript

Narrator: As the last part of his challenge, Dieter asks you to tell him stories you make up yourselves using some of the German words you have learned.

So, go to the back of your activity book and carefully remove the page of cut-out pictures. Use scissors to cut out the individual pictures, then arrange them in the right order on your activity book page to tell a story you make up. Once you have got them all set up in order on your page, tell your story to your mom or dad or your friend, using German words for the pictures.

Any story will be fun! And after you've told your first story a few times, and you can tell it very fast and very well, try a different arrangement with other pictures and tell another story. You can make up as many stories as you like. You might even try letting someone else arrange the pictures and you see if you can tell a story using their arrangement.

Have fun making up your own stories!

Auf Wiedersehen!

This section contains an audio transcript of the adventure story your children will hear on the tape.

Instructions for This Page

Have your children listen carefully as the adventure story is read on the tape.

💡 Encourage your children to take an active part in listening to the adventure story. Ask them to respond to things they hear and have them say out loud words said by the characters on the tape. Younger children might enjoy coloring the picture as the adventure story is read. Older children may want to follow along with the written audio transcript provided in this *Parent's Guide*.

Audio Transcript

🔊 Narrator 2: The Adventure Concludes: Auf Wiedersehen!

Dieter: Very impressive, my young friends. You have indeed made a very good start at learning the German language. I think you now have the tools you need to continue learning German until you someday master it. I'll now give you your last clue, the last piece of your treasure. It is this: Make learning a lifelong habit.

Max: Make learning a lifelong habit.

Narrator: "OK," you say. "I think that makes five now. Build on what you already know, Make learning fun, Don't Stress, Practice, and Make learning a lifelong habit."

Serena: Good memory!

Narrator: *"Danke,"* you reply.

Dieter: Yes, good memory indeed. And now, do you understand this treasure that you have found?

Max: It's a way of learning, I think.

Derek: It is. Go on.

Serena: If we use the treasure, we'll be able to learn lots of good things.

Narrator: "Yeah," you add, "and learning good things is a pretty marvelous treasure all by itself."

Max: Yeah, it is—even if it's not the kind of treasure I thought we were looking for.

Dieter: Very good! I'm glad you have found this treasure, and I'm glad you are beginning to grasp its real worth. I hope you'll use it again and again over the years.

Max & Serena: We will!

Dieter: Excellent. And now, like I said, I you have the tools you need to continue learning German. This is, after all, only the first of many adventures. Power-Glide's adult German course contains

Continued from Children's Activity Book, page 139

another adventure that you are now prepared to start on. I hope you will!

Max: Oh, we will! Don't worry about that, Dieter. Learning German in the valley has been the greatest adventure we've ever had.

Dieter: Excellent, my friends! You've done wonderfully well—*wunderbar!*

Narrator: As Dieter says this, the plane begins to drop down again, and in the distance you can see Max's parents waiting to meet you at the side of a runway. Your plane touches down and a few minutes later you're flooded with warm hellos from Max's parents and warm good-byes from Dieter, who is flying on to the nearby city his business is taking him too. You all wave goodbye and shout *"Auf Wiedersehen!"* as the plane taxis away, with Dieter waving to you out the window. Your week in the valley is over, but you know your German adventures have only just begun.

Semmelknödel—Bread Dumplings

12 hard kaiser rolls diced small

1/2 c butter or margarine

2 T chopped onion

2 T chopped parsley

1 egg

2 c water

1 t salt

2 1/2 c flour

Sauté diced rolls, onions and parsley in butter until bread is crisply toasted. Beat egg, water and salt until frothy. Blend gradually with flour. Add sautéed bread. Mix thoroughly. Makes 8 dumplings. Chill 2 hours to stiffen. With floured hands, shape mixture into dumplings the size of medium oranges. Lower carefully into kettle of boiling salted water. Cook gently, covered, ten minutes. Drain. Serve with meat and gravy dishes, or in soups.

Kartoffelsalat—Potato Salad

1/2 lb bacon (10-12 slices)

1/2 c chopped onion

2 T flour

2 T sugar

1 1/2 t salt

1 t celery seed

1/8 t pepper

1/2 c vinegar

6 c sliced cooked potatoes

2 hard-boiled eggs, sliced

Parsley and pimento

Cook bacon until crisp. Drain and crumble, reserving 2 T bacon fat. Cook onion in reserved fat until tender. Blend in flour, sugar, salt, celery seed, and pepper; add vinegar and 1 cup water; cook and stir until thick and bubbly. Add bacon, potatoes, and eggs; heat thoroughly, tossing lightly. Garnish with parsley, pimento, and bacon curls. Serves 8-10 people.

Wienerschnitzel

When it comes to veal in Austria, it comes to schnitzel

Note: choose quality fine-grained veal or chicken cutlets. Trim all fat, pound each slice as thin as possible, make small cuts around edge so meat won't curl during cooking. Salt.

    2 lbs. veal prepared as above

    1 c flour

    2 eggs beaten with milk, if desired

    1 c bread crumbs

    1 c oil

Dredge veil first in flour, then in eggs (beat in a little milk if needed), and then in bread crumbs. Press the crumbs firmly with palm of hand and shake off excess. Fry in oil deep enough to cover well and so hot that it smokes. Fry each side 2 to 3 minutes, or until golden brown. (Skillet heat is correct when breading surface ripples as it cooks.) Schnitzel is done when a fork goes right through the meat. Drain on a paper towel. Garnish with lemon wedges. Serve with potato salad or cucumber salad.

Apfelstrudel—Apple Strudel

    dough

    strudel filling

    2 c flour

    3 T melted butter

    1/2 c lukewarm water

    3/4 c bread crumbs

    1 egg

    1/2 c sugar

    1 t vegetable oil

    1 T cinnamon

    1/4 t salt

    3 lbs baking apples, peeled and sliced thin

    5 T butter, softened

    3 T melted butter

Sift flour onto large mixing board, heap into a ring. Thoroughly mix water, egg, oil, and salt. Pour mix into center of flour ring a small amount at a time. Work dough until it is a smooth ball. Work one tablespoon of softened butter into dough. Mix very thoroughly. Repeat with remaining tablespoons of softened butter. Work until dough looks smooth and shiny. Set dough in a bowl. Cover with cling wrap, and let rest at least two hours. Generously flour a large pastry cloth.

Set cloth on table or other hard surface. Put dough on cloth, and roll out. Brush with some of melted butter. Put hands under dough, and pull dough in all directions until dough becomes very thin. Be careful not to tear the dough. Cut off thick edges, and use to patch any holes or spots that are too thin. Brush again with melted butter. Lightly brown bread crumbs in melted butter.

Spread mix carefully over two thirds of dough. Spread apples over mix. Combine cinnamon and sugar. Spread cinnamon mix over apples. Lift pastry cloth at filled end of strudel. Gently pull and nudge dough so that strudel begins to roll itself. Pinch ends together and fold them in. Carefully slide strudel onto greased baking sheet. Bake in log shape or carefully shape into horseshoe shape. Brush again with melted margarine. Bake in preheated oven at 425° F for 45 minutes or until golden brown. Brush occasionally with melted butter during baking. Serve warm or cold, dusted with powdered sugar.